The New Evangelization:

Pastoral Reflections on the Sacraments

Rev. Dr. John Arthur Orr

The New Evangelization: Pastoral Reflections on the Sacraments.
Charleston, SC: CreateSpace, 2015.

Orr, John Arthur (1968- ____)

ISBN-13: 978-1517183738
ISBN-10: 1517183731

cum aprobatione superiores
sed
hoc libro, ut omnes tractandi fide ac moribus
ab iudicium Ecclesiae subiecta
secundum canones 824 et 827

Other books by the same author:

Reason in Wojtyla / John Paul II. Charleston, SC:
    CreateSpace, 2014.

*The New Evangelization: Pastoral Reflections on the
    Creed.* Charleston, SC: CreateSpace, 2013.

Dogmatic Questions and Answers for the Year of Faith.
    Charleston, SC: CreateSpace, 2012.

*The Second Vatican Council (1962-1965) and the
    Interpretation of Sacred Scripture.* Charleston, SC:
    CreateSpace, 2011.

Table of Contents

Illustrations

Engravings by Julius Schnorr von Carolsfeld (+1872) first published as *Die Bibel in Bidern* in 1860.

Introduction

As in the earlier volume *The New Evangelization: Pastoral Reflections on the Creed*, this volume collects the various articles based on the *in brief* sections of the *Catechism of the Catholic Church* which were first published at Holy Ghost Catholic Church, Knoxville, Tennessee, in the Sunday *bulletin*. The section on Holy Orders was published between May and August, 2010, during the "Year for Priests" called by Pope Benedict XVI. While the balance were first published from November, 2012 - February 2014. The reference to the passage in the *Catechism* is noted by CCC followed by the article number.

Since the earlier volume was published, Pope Francis has made his contribution to "New Evangelization" studies, especially through his Apostolic Exhortation *Evangelii Gaudium* (24 November, 2013).[1]

---

[1]

http://w2.vatican.va/content/francesco/en/apost_exhortations/documents/papa-francesco_esortazione-ap_20131124_evangelii-gaudium.html (cited on 29 October, 2014; hereafter cited as EG.)

This Apostolic Exhortation, published by Pope Francis, builds upon the XIII Ordinary General Assembly of the Synod of Bishops which met in Rome 7-20 October, 2012. Pope Francis' thought on the "new evangelization" is summarized here.

The basis, source and inspiration of all our efforts in proclaiming the Gospel is the encounter with God's love (EG, 8). As followers of Jesus Christ we have found the source of our "authentic personal fulfilment" and are consequently summoned "to take up the task of evangelization" (EG, 10). Believers, the lukewarm and the non-practicing can all find "new joy in the faith and fruitfulness in the work of evangelization" through a renewal of preaching (EG, 11). Even if the Gospel message is some two thousand years old, "every form of authentic evangelization is always 'new'" (EG, 11). "In every activity of evangelization, the primacy always belongs to God, who has called us to cooperate with Him and who leads us on by the power of His Spirit" (EG, 12).

The newness of the "New Evangelization" "is the newness which God Himself mysteriously brings about and inspires, provokes, guides and accompanies in a thousand ways" (EG, 12). For Pope Francis the "New Evangelization" has everything to do with "the transmission of the faith" (EG, 14-18). The "New Evangelization is a summons addressed to all" (EG, 14). The "New Evangelization is carried out in three principal settings", namely "ordinary pastoral ministry", among "the baptized whose lives do not reflect the demands of Baptism, who lack a meaningful relationship to the Church and no longer experience the consolation born of faith" and to "those who do not know Jesus Christ or who have always rejected Him" (EG, 14-15). Evangelization is first and foremost about preaching the Gospel to those who do not know Jesus Christ or who have always rejected Him" (EG, 15). "Evangelization takes place in obedience to the missionary mandate of Jesus:

> 'Go therefore and make disciples of all nations, baptizing them in the Name of the Father and of the Son and of the Holy Spirit, teaching them to observe all that I have commanded you' (Matthew 28:19-20)" (EG, 19).

"Jesus' command to 'go and make disciples'" is echoed "in the changing scenarios and ever new challenges to the Church's mission of evangelization" to which "all of us are called to take part" (EG, 20). For Pope Francis, "evangelization consists mostly of patience and disregard for constraints of time" (EG, 24). If we as Christ's Church are an "evangelizing community" we will be "filled with joy" knowing "how to rejoice always" celebrating "every small victory, every step forward" (EG, 24). "Evangelization with joy becomes beauty in the liturgy, as part of our daily concern to spread goodness" (EG, 24). At once "the Church evangelizes and is herself evangelized through the beauty of the liturgy, which is both a celebration of the tasks of evangelization and the source of her renewed self-giving" (EG, 24). The "particular Church" (diocese) is "the primary subject of evangelization, since it is the concrete manifestation of the one Church in one specific place, and in it 'the one, holy, catholic, and apostolic Church of Christ is truly present and operative'" (EG, 30; *Cristus Dominus*, 11). Both language and circumstances impact and limit "the task of evangelization" (EG, 45).

An overemphasis on "administering the sacraments apart from other forms of evangelization" as well as an "administrative approach" is seen by Pope Francis as detrimental to a "pastoral approach" (EG, 63). Pope Francis, together with the Synod Fathers, recognizes "great spaces" and the resultant culture as being "a privileged locus of the New Evangelization" (EG, 73). The "New Evangelization" requires the "shedding light" on the "new ways of relating to God, to others and to the world around us and inspiring essential values" reaching "the places where new narratives and paradigms are being formed, bringing the Word of Jesus to the inmost soul of our cities" (EG, 74). It is the Gospel that provides "the best remedy for the ills of our cities" giving a "unified and complete sense of human life" even if a "uniform and rigid program of evangelization is not suited to" the complex reality of urban living (EG, 75). The "'New Evangelization' calls for personal involvement on the part of each of the baptized" (EG, 120). Popular piety too, has been identified by Pope Francis as a *locus theologicus* which demands the attention of all believers engaged in the "New Evangelization" (EG, 126).

It is one thing for us to announce the Gospel, the life, death and resurrection of God Incarnate for our salvation and another for a deep understanding to exist. This is one of the tasks of the "New Evangelization" (cf. EG, 160-175). The proclamation of the Gospel changes not only hearts and minds and lives but also societies and cultures (cf. EG, 176). The "New Evangelization" invites us to "acknowledge the saving power at work" in the lives of the poor and to "put them at the center of the Church's pilgrim way" (EG, 198). The "New Evangelization" calls on every baptized person to be a peacemaker and a credible witness to a reconciled life (EG, 239). To proclaim the Gospel with boldness (*parrhesia*) is one key to the "New Evangelization" (EG, 259-260). Apart from the Blessed Virgin Mary, Mother of God, Mother of the Church, we will never truly understand the spirit of the "New Evangelization" (EG, 284).

As Saint John Paul II and Benedict XVI before him, Pope Francis sees the Blessed Virgin Mary as the "Star of the New Evangelization" (EG, 287-288).[2] Our Lady is the Star of the "New Evangelization" whose intercession we seek for ourselves and the entire Church (EG, 287).[3]

As in the earlier volume *The New Evangelization: Pastoral Reflections on the Creed*[4] this volume includes images which are placed at the beginning of each section, one for each of the seven sacraments, followed by a brief description of the scene as it relates to the sacrament.

---

[2]

For John Paul II: *Ecclesia in America*, (22 January, 1999) 11; *Novo Millennio Ineunte*, (6 January, 2001) 58.3; *Ecclesia in Africa*, (14 September, 1995) 144; *Ecclesia in Asia*, (6 November, 1999) 51.2; For Benedict XVI: *Message to Cardinal Ivan Diaz,* 13 November, 2009; *Message for World Mission Day*, 6 January, 2012; *Message for World Youth Day*, 18 October, 2012.

[3]

For a glimpse into the Mariology of Pope Francis, including his devotion to Mary Undoer of Knots" see: Francis. *The Church of Mercy, A Vision for the Church.* Chicago: Loyola, 2014, 131-143; Sansonetti, Vincenzo. *Pope Francis and the Virgin Mary: A Marian Devotion.* Rizzoli, 2015.

[4] Charleston, SC, CreateSpace, 2013.

viii

Also included is another "Select Bibliography" which builds upon but does not repeat those resources found in the earlier volume. I am grateful to my Bishop, Richard F. Stika of Knoxville, who allowed me a post-doctoral research sabbatical in the first months of this year, when I was able to read many of these resources.

Select Bibliography for the New Evangelization

Burke, Raymond Leo Cardinal. "The New Evangelization and Canon
Law." *Jurist: Studies in Church Order and Ministry* 72:1
(2012) 4-30.

_____. "The new evangelization and sacred music: the unbroken
continuity of holiness, beauty and universality" *Benedict XVI
and beauty in sacred music: proceeding of the third Fota
International Liturgical Conference.* Dublin, Ireland: Four
Courts, 2012, 24-40.

Cahall, Perry. "The Nucleus of the New Evangelization." *Nova et
Vetera* 11:1 (2013) 39-56.

Clark, Edward William. "The New Evangelization and the Formation
of Priests for Today." *Seminary Journal* 18:1 (2012) 5-11.

Dillon, Richard J. "Mark 1:1-15: A 'New Evangelization'?" *Catholic
Biblical Quarterly* 76:1 (January 2014) 1-18.

Driscoll, Jeremy. "Monasticism and the New Evangelization I-II" *The
American Benedictine Review* 4:65 (2014) 372-388, 422-428.

Duncan, Roger. "The Little Flower and the New Evangelization"
Logos: A Journal of Catholic Thought and Culture 3:3
(Summer 2000) 109-123.

Fisichella, Rino. "The New Evangelization I-IV" *The American
Benedictine Review* 4:65 (2014) 353-362, 363-371, 389-401,
422-428.

Gomez, Jose H. "The Formation of Holy Priests and the New
Evangelization." *Seminary Journal* 18:2 (2012) 13-17.

McGregor, Peter John. "New World, New Pentecost, New Church: Pope John Paul II's Understanding of 'New Evangelization'" *Compass* 4 (2012) 18-32.

O'Collins, Gerald. "Will Many Be Saved? What Vatican II Actually Teaches and Its Implications for the New Evangelization" *Pacifica* 27:1 (2014) 111-113.

Pell, George Cardinal. "From Vatican II to the New Evangelization." *Quadrant* 57:3 (March 2013) 66-71.

Prowse, Christopher C. "A New Evangelization for a New World." *Australasian Catholic Record* 89:3 (July 2012) 259-271.

Ramsay, Matthew. "Ex Umbris: Newman's New Evangelization." *New Blackfriars* 93:1045 (May 2012) 339-357.

Rymarz, Richard. "Conversion and the New Evangelization: A Perspective from Lonergan." *Heythrop Journal* 51:5 (September 2010) 753-767.

_____. "The New Evangelization in an Ecclesiological Context." *Heythrop Journal* 52:5 (September 2011) 772-784.

Weinandy, Thomas G. "Will many be saved?: What Vatican II actually teaches and its implications for the new evangelization" *First Things* 229 (January 2013) 61-62.

The baptism of the Lord Jesus by John the Baptist in the Jordan River, when the voice of the Father was heard and the Dove of the Holy Spirit descended upon the Lord who made holy the waters by which we are made holy in saving Baptism. The artist has depicted Saint John the Baptist pouring water (infusion) over the head of the Lord Jesus from a baptismal shell (anacronistic?/!). Note the Lord is not quite knee deep in the Jordan, the Dove is descending, and a crowd of angels and other onlookers are watching (cf. Matthew 3:13-17; Mark 1:9; Luke 3:21-22).

BAPTISM

1.   There are three Sacraments of Christian Initiation: Baptism, Confirmation and Eucharist. The first two, Baptism and Confirmation are not repeated. Regular, worthy reception of Holy Communion, especially at the Sunday Mass each week, helps us to remain and grow in fidelity to Christ, His bride and mystical body the Church, and the graces given in Baptism and Confirmation. While each of these three (3) Sacraments of Christian Initiation are treated separately in the *Catechism*, together they complete and perfect our belonging to Christ.

Baptism is the Sacrament of Christian Initiation which begins our new life in Christ. There are twenty verses in the New Testament which make mention of 'Baptism' and eight which refer to 'baptize.' The Greek transliterations are: *baptizo, baptisma, baptismos*, refer to washings.

The Lord Jesus rebuked many of the Pharisees and Sadducees, who had gone to see Saint John the Baptizer who called them "a brood of vipers," wanting to know who had warned them to "flee from the wrath to come." Before Baptism we retain Original Sin which we inherit and any sins we may have committed, abusing our free will. These make us worse than a brood of vipers, but God's saving graces, freely given in Baptism, cleanse us from all sin. Penance and repentance of sin are also part of the approach to and fidelity to Baptism (cf. Matthew 3:5-8; Mark 1:4; Luke 3:3). In responding to the query of the Chief Priests, Scribes, and the Elders about His authority, Jesus asked them about "the baptism of John," whether it was "from Heaven or from men" (cf. Matthew 21:23-27; Mark 11:27-33; Luke 20:1-8). Both Jesus' Baptism and authority are greater than that of John (cf. Matthew 3:11; John 5:36). Jesus likens His Passion to baptism when speaking with James and John (cf. Mark 10:35-40; Luke 12:50). The Church has considered a "Baptism of Blood" to have been received by those who have died as martyrs even before they were Baptized in water.

Confirmation is the Sacrament of Christian Initiation which affirms our life in Christ. With a fresh outpouring of the Holy Spirit, complementing the initial outpouring given in saving Baptism. Whenever any of us sin, mortally or venially, we turn our backs on God and His saving will. By repentance and conversion we reaffirm God's choice in our favor. The graces of Confirmation strengthen our bond with Christ and His Church.

The Eucharist is the Sacrament of Christian Initiation which nourishes us as disciples of Christ with His Body and Blood in view of our transformation in Christ. The adage, 'you are what you eat' comes to mind here. The more we are united to the Lord in Holy Communion, the better we may be His disciples, leading others to Him. (cf. CCC, 1275)

4

2.   When reflecting on Holy Baptism, the *Catechism* cites the "Great Commission" given by the Lord Jesus Himself: "Go, therefore, to all nations, make disciples, baptize them in the Name of the Father and of the Son and of the Holy Spirit, and teach them to do all that I have commanded you" (Matthew 28:19-20).

There are at least six (6) things we should consider here.

First, when the Lord gives these directions He is not limiting His plan to the generation or the location immediately known to Him during His earthly ministry. Rather, He says: "Go to all nations." This means that the Holy Gospel is for all peoples in every place. The faith is not just for the Middle East, nor for North America but every continent, every nation...

A second consideration concerns the Lord's direction to "make disciples." When we introduce people to Christ the Lord, His Gospel, His Church, we do so that they might become His disciples as we have already become. The Greek words *mathetes, manthano* translate variously: to become a pupil, to enrol as a scholar, one who is taught or instructed and are always contrasted with the master or teacher.

The Greek word *didasko* is better translated as "to teach." Jesus Christ came from Heaven to Earth to teach us about God and about ourselves, made in the Divine Image, redeemed by the Blood of the Lamb in which we are washed and saved.

A third consideration has to do with what follows our having learned what the Lord has taught us through His bride and mystical body, Mother Church, namely to be baptized. The Greek word *baptizo* refers to washing and bathing. In the case of the Sacrament of Baptism it is a washing away of Original Sin and any other sins committed before Holy Baptism.

A fourth consideration to make concerns the waters being poured on the candidate or the candidate being immersed in the waters while the *Trinitarian* formula, "In the Name of the Father and of the Son and of the Holy Spirit," is pronounced, preceded by the effective utterance "I baptize you" or "be baptized." The Name of God is one even though the Divine Persons are three. We are made adopted sons and daughters in the Son by the outpouring of the Spirit, able to call God our Father, thanks to the special graces of this sacrament.

6

A fifth consideration echos being made a disciple. In order for us to learn we must be taught. What and Who is taught is Jesus Christ Himself.

A sixth consideration follows from having been made a disciple, having been taught and baptized: we are to do all that the Lord Jesus has prescribed. We are to turn away from sin. We are to love our enemies. (cf. CCC, 1276)

3.   Some of our non-Catholic neighbors are very fond of asking "Have you been born again?" As followers of Jesus Christ in His Holy Catholic Church we can answer a definitive "yes" to this question if we have been baptized. To be "born again" by water and the Spirit is to fulfill the teaching of the Lord Jesus Christ which he shared late one night with Nicodemus (cf. John 3:4-12).

The Sacrament of Baptism is so important to the Lord Jesus that He orders it to be administered as part of His departing words to the Apostles: Go therefore, teach all nations, baptizing them in the Name of the Father and of the Son and of the Holy Spirit (cf. Matthew 28:19). This directive applies to us also, not just the Apostles. One important thing we are to teach is the importance and necessity of Baptism.

Baptism is necessary for salvation according to the Lord's will: "Unless a man be born of water and of the Spirit, he cannot enter into the Kingdom of God"(John 3:5). The Greek word *ean me* translates variously as: "if not" or "unless" or "before" or "except." We enter the Kingdom of God, the Church, even in the here and now through holy Baptism. When Jesus says: "He that believes and is baptized shall be saved, but he that believes not shall be condemned" we should take it seriously for He is the "way, the truth, and the life" and the "truth will set us free," including the truth of the importance and necessity of Holy Baptism (cf. Mark 16:16; John 8:32; 14:6).

The Church also is necessary for salvation according to the Lord's will. This is because it is from Mother Church that we receive Holy Baptism. We receive Holy Baptism from Mother Church because Christ the Lord has entrusted His sacraments, Baptism included, to her. Holy Mother Church is also necessary for salvation insofar as the Lord Jesus has committed His Gospel to her, to continue His teaching ministry even until He returns at the end of the ages to judge the living and the dead (cf. Acts 10:42; 2 Timothy 4:1-5; 1 Peter 4:5-6). Each of us will be judged not only according to our deeds but also to the extent that we have kept and shared the faith delivered once to all the saints (cf. Romans 2:6; Jude 1:3). When we live holy lives we are living by God's grace and are being faithful to our Baptism wherein Satan, all his empty works and the glamour of evil were renounced. True love of neighbor will seek to extend the blessing of faith to all we meet, that they too may enjoy friendship with God, divine adoption through Baptism and the life of grace. (cf. CCC, 1277)

4.   Each of the sacraments have that which is particular to them. An example from the Eucharist would include the necessary matter of wheat bread and wine vinted from the grape. This is called the 'matter' of the Eucharist.   These words are the 'form' of the Eucharist. Besides the necessary bread and wine, there must also be a validly ordained priest to pronounce the words of consecration "this is My body... this is My blood..." in order for the transubstantiation to occur.

Holy Baptism also has it's essential matter and form: water and the Trinitarian formula. Without these, the intention to baptize, and an unbaptized person who is willing - either personally or through proxies (parents and godparents), to be baptized, there is no Baptism. The specific matter and form of Baptism are our concern here.

The proper matter for Holy Baptism is water into which the candidate is either plunged or has poured out especially on the head.

10

The natural cleansing properties of water are carried over to the spiritual sphere. Instead of dirt, grass stains and the like we are cleansed in saving Baptism from the stains of Original Sin, which we inherit, and from the sins we have actually committed, mortal (serious, grave) or venial (committed without full knowledge, full consent, less serious).

The proper form for Holy Baptism is the pronounced invocation of the Most Holy Trinity with the effective utterance being either "N., I baptize you in the Name of the Father and of the Son and of the Holy Spirit" or "N., be baptized in the Name of the Father and of the Son and of the Holy Spirit." An 'effective utterance' in civil matters or worldly concerns is discernable when a Sheriff's Deputy or Police Officer says "you are under arrest" we are in fact, under arrest. Or when the judge says "you are free to go" we are in fact, free to go. These examples of 'effective utterances' are not unrelated to the form of the sacraments. When the saving waters are poured and the invocation is pronounced, we are baptized.

When the words of consecration are spoken by the priest at Holy Mass the bread and wine are changed into Christ, body, blood, soul and divinity.

Some people, trying to be more clever than Mother Church, thought it would be good to change the words, the form, of Baptism. Rather than invoking "the Father and the Son and the Holy Spirit" these folks (heretics) invoked "the Creator, the Redeemer, and the Sanctifier."
This is not in conformity with either Jesus' specific instructions or with the requirements of the Church. These "baptisms" were and are invalid. Each of the Divine Persons of the Trinity are active in creation, redemption and sanctification, not just one or another. (cf. CCC, 1278)

5.   There are at least eight fruits or graces especially linked to the Sacrament of Baptism in the *Catechism*. Here we consider them, each individually, in order to have a better grasp on the rich reality which is Baptism.

12

Baptism gives us the remission of Original Sin. While none of us committed the first sin, we have inherited its effects with our human nature. The sad temporal consequences of Original Sin remain in us, even after Baptism: suffering, death, ignorance and a tendency to sin (concupiscence). The eternal consequences of Original Sin, separation from God are washed away. Christian Baptism is prepared for by Saint John the Baptist who preached both baptism and the forgiveness of sins (cf. Mark 1:4; Luke 3:3).

Baptism also gives us the remission of all personal sins committed up to the point of Baptism. Christian preaching is directed to repentance and the forgiveness of sins, beginning with Holy Baptism (cf. Luke 24:47; Acts 2:38).

Baptism gives us supernaturally new life in Christ. When Jesus spoke with Nicodemus late one night (cf. John 3:1-21) it was not only about the necessity of Baptism (v. 5) but also about everlasting life (v. 16) and the new birth given through the saving waters (v.4-7).

Without specifically mentioning Baptism, Saint Peter does address our being "born again, not of corruptible seed, but incorruptible, by the Word of God who lives and remains forever" (1 Peter 1:23). Being baptized into Christ's death also gives access to riseing anew with Him (cf. Romans 6:3-4).

Baptism is the sacrament of divine adoption, wherein we are made adopted sons and daughters in the one only eternal Son of the eternal Father (cf. Romans 8:29; Ephesians 1:5).

Baptism makes us members of Christ (1 Corinthians 6:25; 12:27). The Lord Jesus teaches us that without Him we can do nothing (cf. John 15:5). It is *via* grace, faith, and Baptism that we are with Jesus, in whom we live and move and have our being (cf. Acts 17:28).

Baptism makes us temples of the Holy Spirit (1 Corinthians 3:16-17; 6:19; 2 Corinthians 6:16). As we honor the Parish Church and the diocesan Cathedral Church because they are consecrated places of worship and places of reservation of our Lord in the Blessed Sacrament, so too, each of the baptized has been consecrated and set apart for God, who dwells within us by His grace.

Baptism incorporates us into the Church, the Body of Christ (Romans 12:5). Because the Holy Spirit is the soul of the Church, we are at the same time living stones of this spiritual house (cf. 1 Peter 2:5).

Baptism also makes us participants who share in the priesthood of Christ offering up spiritual sacrifices (1 Peter 2:5). (cf. CCC, 1279)

6.   An indelible spiritual sign, also called a 'character,' is imprinted on the soul by Baptism. This is the sure and certain teaching of the Church. There are two (2) difficulties associated with speaking this way: first, the soul is immaterial; and second, how can a 'mark' (something visible) be made on what is immaterial or invisible? Even though the rational spiritual soul of the human being is both immaterial and invisible it is real, contrary to the dictates of empiricism (which state that only that which can be touched, weighed, measured... is real). Life, locomotion, intelligence, communication and abstraction, to name a few, manifest the human soul.

An analogy frequently given to describe the indelible spiritual sign given in Baptism is the impression made in wax by a signet ring which does not change the quantity of wax while leaving a mark. Confirmation and Holy Orders also impart indelible spiritual signs on those who validly receive them.

The baptismal character consecrates the baptized person to the cult of Christian religion. To be consecrated is to be set apart for God, who is all Holy (1 Peter 1:15; Revelation 4:8). The Greek word *hagiazo* and the Hebrew words *haram* and *kadhesh* are translated as consecrate and sanctify. There are various consecrations in the Christian religion, people are consecrated in Baptism, Confirmation, Holy Orders. Husbands and wives are consecrated in Marriage. Bread and wine are consecrated at the Holy Mass...

Baptism is not able to be repeated due to the lasting spiritual sign, the character, imparted by the sacrament. Saint Paul, inspired by God, instructs us in this way: "One Lord, one faith, one baptism" (cf. Ephesians 4:5). There are two (2) other sacraments which keep us faithful to our Baptism once received: Penance and Eucharist.

These are each treated specifically in the *Catechism*. These three (3)

sacraments, Baptism, Eucharist and Penance, are all embedded in the

Lord's Prayer: Baptism allows us to call God our Father in light of

the divine adoption; the Eucharist is our supersubstantial daily bread

from Heaven; our trespasses are forgiven in the Sacrament of Penance

(cf. Matthew 6:9-13; Luke 11:2-4).

Saint Augustine (*Contra Epist. Parmen*, ii; *On Baptism,* 5:23),

Saint Basil (*Sermons on Moral and Practical Subjects*, 13:5), and

Saint Cyril of Jerusalem (*Catechetical Lectures*, 3:10, 12) among

others, all understood the true teaching regarding holy Baptism as

being that once it is validly conferred, Baptism can never be repeated.

Saint Thomas Aquinas for his part addresses the indelible seal or

character in ST III, Q. 63, A.1-6. The character is imparted or

produced in the soul by the grace of the sacraments of Baptism,

Confirmation and Holy Orders. These teachings were then taken up by

the Fathers of the Council of Trent (Session VII, canon ix). (cf. CCC,

1280)

7.   Baptism, as all the sacraments, has to do with salvation. Our lives in Christ begin with Holy Baptism. Because there are those who have not yet received or approached the saving waters of Baptism the Fathers of the Second Vatican Council (1962-1965) addressed the issue in the *Constitution on the Church, Lumen Gentium*, 16. The *Catechism* similarly addresses the issue. While not using the specific terms "Baptism of Desire," "Baptism of Blood," here the *Catechism* in treating the Sacrament of Baptism seems to have them in mind. What is a "Baptism of Desire"? What is a "Baptism of Blood"? A tension exists between the necessity of Baptism (cf. John 3:5-7; Mark 16:16----) on the one hand and God's universal salvific will (cf. John 3:17; Romans 11:26; 1 Corinthians 10:33; 1 Timothy 2:3-4) on the other.

        God is God and can save and will save whomever He will. The ordinary way God saves us is through the life of grace lived within Church, beginning with Baptism. Catechumens are those who are preparing for the Sacraments of Initiation (Baptism, Confirmation, Eucharist).

These people clearly desire to receive the Sacrament of Baptism and, *ecclesia supplet* (the Church suppling) sees the saving grace of God already at work in them, even should they sadly die before actually receiving Holy Baptism. Part of any "Baptism of Desire" includes a "sincere search for God." If one is living without any seeking for whatever is good or true or beautiful, (cf. Philippians 4:8-9) all of which come from and lead back to God, then one may not be actually or sincerely searching for God. It is not enough for the unbaptized to only sincerely seek God, who has sought us out in Christ, but they must also (as must the baptized) exert themselves in accomplishing the Divine Will (think here of the Ten Commandments and all their parts, the Natural Law). If we willfully do evil and willfully do not repent salvation is forfeited. But, if moved by God's grace, and that is the only way any of us keep God's commandments, then, in His mercy and mysterious providence, God may save us even beyond the sacramental system He set up, beginning with Baptism. While God's preferred way to administer the graces we need to be holy and pleasing in His sight, the Spirit breathes as He wills (cf. John 3:8).

Those who tragically suffer martyrdom, who are killed because of their faith in Christ, even before they might receive Baptism (think here of Saint John the Baptist [29 August] and the Holy Innocents [28 December]) are saved by God's grace in what has been called a 'Baptism of Blood.' Jesus spoke of His death and the martyrdom of His Apostles as a sort of baptism (cf. Mark 10:38-39). (cf. CCC, 1281)

8.   There are some people who have refused to have their children baptized, saying "I will let them make their own decision." Consistency would require such parents to also let their children decide whether or not to go to the pediatrician, dentist or school. To bring the child to the saving waters is good spiritual healthcare, safeguarding from the infection of sin allows the child to learn in the school of the Lord's service.

That the Sacrament of Baptism has been administered to children even in ancient times appears evident in view of Scripture which teaches that Lydia and "her household" were baptized upon hearing the preaching of Saint Paul (cf. Acts 16:15) as was the "household of Stephanus" (cf. 1 Corinthians 1:16). My brother's household includes his wife and their children, my nieces and nephew. Refusal of Baptism to infants or children would be to discount them from the household of believers.

The Lord Jesus teaches us that we are to become like little children that we might enter the Kingdom of Heaven (cf. Matthew 18:3). Baptism is the sacrament whereby we enter Mother Church and are made adopted children of the eternal heavenly Father and citizens of the heavenly Kingdom. The Lord Jesus Himself did not forbid the children to come to Him, rather He teaches us that His Kingdom is for such as them (cf. Matthew 19:13-14; Mark 10:13-14; Luke 18:16). It would thwart the plan of God by refusing children Jesus' saving waters. It was the desire of the Lord Jesus to gather the children of Jerusalem as a hen gathers her chicks (cf. Matthew 23:37).

Jesus gathers us to Himself and His mystical body the Church through Baptism.

What better gifts might parents give to their children than the gifts of grace and faith and redemption and divine adoption all of which come through the Sacrament of Baptism (cf. Matthew 7:11; Luke 11:13)? What parents would not want their children to be equal to the angels and children of God (cf. Luke 20:36)? In Baptism we are made higher than the angels, not only citizens of Heaven, not merely creatures, but adopted children of God. To disallow children who have Original Sin or any others who are repentant access to the saving waters of Baptism would be to despise Christ, His bath of new life (cf. Luke 10:16).

We enter into Christian life in the Church, pillar and bulwark of the truth, by Baptism and are baptized into Christ Jesus who is Himself, the way, the truth and the life who sets us free to act in freedom as children of God (cf. John 8:32; 14:6; Romans 8:21; Galatians 3:26; 4:31; Ephesians 4:5; 1 Timothy 3:15). (cf. CCC, 1282)

9.   There are three sorts of Baptism which should be considered: the actual Sacrament of Baptism, with the pouring of or immersing in water together with the words "I baptize you in the Name of the Father, and of the Son, and of the Holy Spirit"; the "baptism of blood" undergone by those who suffer martyrdom before they were sacramentally baptized (Saint John the Baptist and the Holy Innocents come to mind here); and finally the "baptism of desire" which may possibly be related to those who die without either the actual Sacrament of Baptism or the "baptism of blood."

Those who may have received the "baptism of desire" can include those children who sadly die before Holy Baptism and those catechumens who die before they receive the sacraments of initiation, including Baptism. These people were actually preparing for the saving waters, they wanted to be baptized. When considering the little children, the desire was on the part of the parents who want what is best for their children. There is nothing greater than God, and Holy Baptism incorporates us into the very mystery and life of the Trinity, God, Father, Son and Spirit.

In the Funeral Liturgy for children who die without sacramental Baptism the faithful are invited to have confidence in God's mercy. God knows the desires of our hearts and His mysterious ways are beyond our understanding. Those weighed down by grief at the loss of a child seek to find reassurances of God's infinite goodness. God knows that these parents would have baptized their child in a timely fashion. There is nothing which can be done to earn or deserve God's grace and mercy. God's grace and mercy are gifts freely given and freely received, including the gift of salvation. Those children younger than seven (7) who sadly die without the Sacrament of Baptism only have the stain of Original Sin upon them. They did not commit Original Sin, it has been inherited. This is one reason for confidence in God's mercy. There are others.

The importance of Baptism is key here, as is our fidelity to the saving waters. The Lord Jesus reminds us of the importance of doing the will of the Father so as to enter into the Kingdom of Heaven (cf. Matthew 7:21-23).

Holy Baptism is part of the Father's will for us, made known by the Lord Jesus Himself (Matthew 28:19; Mark 16:16).

Anyone who gets to Heaven, gets there in God's mercy. We are to pray not only for our own souls, our own salvation, but for everyone, even our enemies (cf. Matthew 5:44; Luke 6:27-28, 35; Acts 8:22; James 5:16). All the more are we to pray for the salvation of the little ones who were not baptized (cf. John 3:5). (cf. CCC, 1283)

10.   In cases of necessity one may baptize anyone who has not already been baptized who is not opposed to being baptized. A case of necessity is surely already present when someone who has not been baptized is in danger of death. This often may happen in delivery rooms with sickly newborns or at accident scenes. There was a time when doctors, nurses and emergency personnel were all taught how to administer Holy Baptism in cases of necessity. Actually, all of the faithful should know how to baptize in cases of emergency.

While the ordinary minister of the Sacrament of Baptism is a Bishop, Priest or Deacon , in cases of necessity, one may validly administer this sacrament, even someone who is not a Christian. Even if the person doing the baptizing is a notorious criminal, atheist or the like, they may validly baptize so long as they meet a three-fold requirement: 1st have the intention of doing what the Church does when administering Baptism; 2nd pour water on the head of the candidate while; 3rd saying "I baptize you in the Name of the Father, the Son and the Holy Spirit."

The "intention of doing what the Church does" is namely to wash away Original Sin, make one an adopted child of God and member of the Church. The pouring of the water and the invocation of the Holy Trinity, naming each Divine Person individually are to occur simultaneously. The water is not to be poured only over the feet or hands but must, at least, be poured over the head.

The reason why Mother Church insists on the importance and necessity of Baptism flow from the very words of Christ Jesus, spoken to Nicodemus:

> "Amen, amen, I say to you, unless a man be born again of water and the Holy Spirit, he cannot enter into the Kingdom of God" (John 3:5).

The reason why Mother Church insists on the importance and necessity of the baptismal formula, again, also flow from the very words of Christ Jesus in His *great commission*: "Go therefore, teach all nations, baptizing in the Name of the Father and of the Son and of the Holy Spirit. Teach them to observe all things whatsoever I have commanded you. And behold, I am with you all days, even to the consummation of the world" (Matthew 28:19-20).

There are both rights and responsibilities flowing from Baptism. This is why under less dire circumstances a suitable period of Christian formation (catechesis) precedes Baptism. On the day of Pentecost Saint Peter delivered to great effect a brief catechesis resulting in the Baptism of three thousand souls (cf. Acts 2:1-41).

We see another very brief catechesis presented by Saint Philip followed immediately by the administration of Baptism in Acts 8:26-39. (cf. CCC, 1284)

Fifty days after Easter the Holy Spirit as if tongues of fire descended upon the Apostles gathered in the upper room. Confirmation has been likened to a personal Pentecost, when the Holy Spirt comes upon each of us that we might hear the Gospel, and live the Gospel, and share the Gospel with boldness like the Apostles before us (cf. Acts 2:1-4; 19:2; 1 Corinthians 6:19).

CONFIRMATION

1.   To begin summarizing the second of the three Sacraments of

Initiation, Confirmation, the *Catechism* cites Sacred Scripture:

> "Hearing that Samaria had welcomed the Word of God the
> Apostles who were in Jerusalem sent Peter and John. These
> went down therefore to the Samaritans and prayed for them,
> that finally the Holy Spirit would be given to them. Because
> He had not yet fallen on any one of them, they had only been
> baptized in the Name of the Lord Jesus. Then Peter and John
> aimed at imposing their hands and they received the Holy
> Spirit" (Acts 8:14-17).

Part of Confirmation is the welcoming of the Word of God.

This is at least two-fold: welcoming the Word of God in Sacred

Scripture; welcoming the Word of God who is Christ Jesus the Lord,

the Word made flesh (cf. John 1:14).

Another part of Confirmation is the link with the Apostolic

Church, here represented by the Apostles Peter and John. The local

Bishop is the Successor of the Apostles in our midst. Bishops are (in

the Western / Latin Church) the ordinary ministers of the Sacrament of

Confirmation.

In order for the Apostles Peter and John to confer the Sacrament of Confirmation upon the Samaritans, they first prayed for them. This holds in the current rite of Confirmation. The Sacrament of Confirmation is normally administered within the context of the Holy Mass, one of our greatest prayers. There are specific prayers prayed during the Mass wherein one is confirmed, while other prayers at the same Mass are silent. The Bishop prays a specific consecratory prayer calling upon God to send the Spirit upon those to be confirmed: A Spirit of Wisdom, of Understanding, of Counsel, of Fortitude, of Knowledge, of Godliness, and of Fear of the Lord (cf. Isaiah 11:2-3). These have been identified as the "Gifts of the Holy Spirit."

The Holy Spirit is at work in Holy Baptism, when we receive the gifts of Faith, Hope and Love (cf. 1 Corinthians 13:13), and it is the Holy Spirit who allows us to call out "Abba Father" and "Jesus is Lord" (cf. Romans 8:15; 1 Corinthians 12:3) there is yet a further outpouring of the Holy Spirit in the Sacrament of Confirmation as we are reminded in Acts 8.

It is one thing to be Baptized in the Name of the Lord Jesus (together with the Father and the Holy Spirit [cf. Matthew 28:19]) it is another thing to be Confirmed and sealed with the gift of the Holy Spirit. Confirmation presupposes Baptism.

The imposition of hands by the Bishop in the Sacrament of Confirmation should remind us of the Apostles Peter and John imposing hands upon the Samaritans as they received the Holy Spirit. May the Holy Spirit make us all holy. (cf. CCC, 1315)

2.   There are six (6) specific graces of Confirmation identified by the *Catechism* which we consider each in turn.

The first grace of Confirmation is the perfection of the grace of Baptism. Baptism is only the first of the three Sacraments of Initiation. Together with Confirmation and Holy Communion or Eucharist are we made complete members of Christ's mystical body on Earth, the Church. Baptism and Confirmation are not repeated, but regular and worthy reception of Holy Communion will keep us faithful to the graces received in Baptism and Confirmation.

The second grace of Confirmation is to root us more profoundly in divine filiation. This way the divine adoption we receive in Baptism is solidified all the more. We are adopted sons and daughters of God in the one only Son, Jesus Christ.

The third grace of Confirmation incorporates us more firmly in Christ. While we belong to Christ by the grace of Baptism, this further grace is like so much more supernatural cement.

The fourth grace of Confirmation makes our tie with the Church more solid. While the tie we have with Christ Himself and His bride, Mother Church, through Holy Baptism is solid, it is often made on our behalf through the proxy of our parents and Godparents for those who are baptized as infants. When the Sacrament of Confirmation is separated from Baptism as it is by and large, in the Latin West, the reaffirmation of the Faith engages the will of the confirmand anew.

The fifth grace of Confirmation associates us more with the mission of the Church.

34

While we participate in the life and mission of the Holy Church through Holy Baptism, we do so all the more through the graces of Confirmation. An older rite of Confirmation includes at the sign of peace a ceremonial 'slap' to remind the confirmand of the sufferings which may accompany the spread and defense of the Faith which is a part of the responsibilities assumed by Confirmation.

The sixth grace of Confirmation helps us to render witness to the Christian Faith through our words and deeds. Without the special graces of God our words and deeds fall short. With the graces God gives in Confirmation we are able to conform our will, our words and our deeds to God's will and Word. If all we do is talk about God and never talk to God (pray) there is something wrong. If all we do is exhort sinners to stop sinning while we continue all the while steeped in sin there is something wrong (cf. Mark 1:15; Luke 17:4; John 5:14; 8:11, 34; 9:41; Romans 3:9; 6:1-2, 11-23; 11:26). Confirmation calls us to correspondence between the Faith professed and the Faith lived and the Faith shared once for all (cf. Jude 1:3). (cf. CCC, 1316)

3.   Jesus Christ established His one only Church during His earthly life and ministry. Jesus Christ also instituted the Seven Sacraments which He entrusted to His Church for our salvation and growth in holiness and grace. Certain sacraments are able to be received only one time due to the specific graces they give (cf. Ephesians 4:5). Baptism and Confirmation both impart an 'indelible character' or 'spiritual sign' upon the soul, marking us as belonging to God in a special way (cf. 2 Corinthians 1:22; Ephesians 4:30).

I once heard the Bishop of Tyler, Texas, speaking to young people from his diocese about the permanent mark given in these sacraments, like the branding of cattle. There are, of course, differences: sacraments are for people (not bovines); the brand on a steer passes with the decay of the creature while to our glory in Heaven or our shame in Hell the character given in Baptism and Confirmation endures for all eternity.

Another consideration might include indelible laundry markers, like those used to identify your laundry when going to summer camp.

The difference between the marks made in the sacraments of Baptism and Confirmation are spiritual and enduring, while those made with the laundry pen last only as long as the garment.

In order that we might recognize His Church throughout the ages Christ the Lord established His Church with distinguishing marks: One, Holy, Catholic, Apostolic. So too we are each individually marked by His sacraments which identify us as belonging to Him. Consider some other distinguishing features: 'golden arches' for the hungry, an apple with a bite out of it for the computer savvy or the juxtaposed letters VW for the automobile. When we see these we know what to expect. The good God likewise has expectations when it comes to His creatures. When God's expectations are even greater when He sees our souls, marked by His grace through Baptism and Confirmation. God gives to the baptized and confirmed the graces needed to correspond to His holy and saving will for us. Those who conform their lives to God's holy will recognize the words of the Gospel: "Good and faithful servant, because you have been faithful... enter into the joy of the Lord" (cf. Matthew 25:21).

The contrary is no less true. Those who spurn, reject and refuse to conform their lives to God's holy will have a different fate: "be cast out into the exterior darkness, where there shall be weeping and gnashing of teeth" (cf. Matthew 25:31).

The singular graces given in Baptism and Confirmation are enduring, able to be called upon throughout our lives, renewed by our fidelity to the Eucharist and Penance worthily received. Baptism and Confirmation set us apart, consecrated to the service of the Lord alone (cf. Galatians 2:19). (cf. CCC, 1317)

4.   While the number of the sacraments, seven, are the same throughout the entire Church, East and West, sacramental discipline differs somewhat. When it comes to Confirmation, the Sacred Chrism - the holy oil mixed with balsam and blessed by the Bishop during Holy Week is the same, and the imposition of hands is the same. What differs is the timing of the administration and the minister, and the name of the sacrament.

The question as to when to administer the Sacrament of Confirmation is answered differently in the different Rites of the Church. The Latin West focuses on the "age of reason" normally thought to be about seven years of age and is the same requirement for the reception of Holy Communion for the first time. This way the recipient has a certain amount of understanding when approaching and receiving the sacraments. The Greek East focuses rather on the givenness of the sacraments and how there is nothing which can be done to deserve God's freely given grace. This is made obvious by the reception of all three Sacraments of Initiation at once in the East, even in infancy.

In the Latin West the ordinary minister of the Sacrament of Confirmation is the Bishop. Reservation of the administration of Confirmation to the Bishop highlights the bond which the confirmand (person receiving Confirmation) has with the Church, represented in a special way by the Bishop.

Extraordinarily in the Latin West a Priest may administer the Sacrament of Confirmation, normally only at the Easter Vigil or in cases when there is the immediate danger of death. By contrast, in the Greek East, Priests using the Sacred Chrism blessed by the Bishop are the ordinary minister of the Sacrament of Confirmation.

Confirmation should also be considered in conjunction with the other two Sacraments of Initiation, Baptism and Eucharist. While Baptism and Confirmation are not to be repeated, due to the character which they impart, it is the worthy and frequent reception of the Holy Eucharist which keeps us faithful to Baptism and Confirmation.

In the Latin West this sacrament is called 'Confirmation' in that the truth and correctness of our profession of faith is asserted anew in a formal, definite way. The Latin word *confirmare* from which is derived the English word 'confirm' is itself based on the Latin word *firmus* meaning 'firm.'

This is echoed throughout the Sacred Scriptures in which God calls us to 'stand firm in the faith' (1 Peter 5:9) and to be strengthened as disciples and encouraged, remaining 'true to the faith' (cf. Acts 14:22) and even that our faith in Christ is to be firm (cf. Colossians 2:5). In the Greek East this sacrament is known as 'Chrismation,' taking its name from the Holy Oil, Sacred Chrism. (cf. CCC, 1318)

5.   For those who are not confirmed in infancy, as in the Eastern Rites of the Catholic Church, there are six (6) requirements for Confirmation identified in the *Catechism of the Catholic Church*. Various Dioceses and Parishes often impose even further requirements.

The first requirement for the Confirmation of those not confirmed as infants is the attainment of the age of reason. This is normally recognized as being around seven (7) years or age, when one may discern right from wrong.

The second requirement for the Confirmation of those not confirmed as infants is the Profession of Faith.

When infants are baptized and confirmed the faith is professed for them, on their behalf, by their parents and godparents.

The third requirement for the Confirmation of those not confirmed as infants is being in the "state of grace." The saving waters of Baptism cleanse us of Original Sin. When we sin mortally after Baptism (doing something seriously wrong as made known by the Commandments of God and all their parts, knowingly, without coercion or willfully) we abandon the state of grace. Sin is an abuse of our free will. Living holy lives, thanks to God's grace and mercy is to live in the freedom of the children of God (cf. Romans 8:21). In order to assume the responsibilities demanded by the Sacrament of Confirmation we should be well confessed. Blessed John Paul II (1978-2005) is said to have gone to Confession each week so as to be in a state of grace.

The fourth requirement for the Confirmation of those not confirmed as infants is to have the intention to receive the sacrament. Here the Church calls forth from those who are able to give consent to do so. No one forced God to make us or to redeem us.

God has made us with free will and calls for our acceptance of His revelation to likewise be free.

The fifth requirement for the Confirmation of those not confirmed as infants is preparedness to assume the role of a disciple of Christ. Religious education programs in our Catholic Schools and Parish Schools of Religion (PSR) or the Confraternity of Christian Doctrine (CCD) and the Rite of Christian Initiation for Adults (RCIA) all help those preparing for Confirmation to be ready to assume the role of discipleship. The disciples of Christ know Him and His teachings. Disciples of Christ know and love Him, His doctrine, His Gospel...

The sixth and final requirement for the Confirmation of those not confirmed as infants is preparedness to assume the role of a witness of Christ. Discipleship leads to witness. The Greek words *martus, martur* are the roots of our English word martyr and translate as "witness."

Both discipleship and witness are carried out in the "ecclesial community" (the Church) and in "temporal affairs" (the world). (cf. CCC, 1319)

6.   The essential rite of Confirmation includes both matter and form. The matter of Confirmation is the anointing with Holy Chrism. Chrism is the perfumed oil used in Baptism, Confirmation, priestly and episcopal Ordination, as well as the consecration of Churches and Altars. Chrisim is consecrated by the Bishop during Holy Week at the Mass of the Chrism. The form of Confirmation includes both a gesture and words spoken by the minister. Interesting here, the *Catechism* includes the practice of both the East and West, reminding us of the universality of the Church.

There are two different customs concerning the anointing with Holy Chrism in the Sacrament of Confirmation. In the West, the anointing with Holy Chrism is made on the forehead.

44

This single, simple anointing, corresponds well with the Roman

Liturgy which has a certain directness and noble simplicity, even if it

tends to the cerebral.

In the East, the anointing with Holy Chrism is made on the

forehead and the organs of the senses, such as the eyes, nose, ears,

mouth... This more baroque anointing reminds us that God does not

limit His grace only to our minds but even to all the senses which feed

the mind

In both the East and West the imposition of hands takes place

in the Sacrament of Confirmation. Each of the sacraments invoke the

Holy Spirit, through this *epicletic* gesture (the imposition of hands).

Sacred Scripture presents the imposition of hands in relation to

blessings and the transmission of the Spirit and worship (cf. Matthew

19:13; Acts 8:17; 28:8; 1 Timothy 5:22; Exodus 29:10, 15, 19).

The form or words used to signify the Sacrament of

Confirmation are similar yet distinct in both the East and the West.

The eastern Byzantine Rite uses the form: 'Receive the mark of the gift of the Holy Spirit,' while the Roman Rite uses the form: 'Be sealed with the gift of the Holy Spirit.' 'The gift of the Holy Spirit' is the same in both rites. To be marked and to be sealed are not unrelated. A mark was put on Cain as a sign of divine protection (cf. Genesis 4:15). Ezekiel was directed by God to mark the foreheads of those who sighed and mourned for the abominations committed in the land (cf. Ezekiel 9:4). Jezebel, the wife of Ahab, sealed letters with his ring, identifying them as his (cf. 1 Kings 21:7-8). Letters written on behalf of king Ahasuerus were also sealed with his ring to show they belong to him (cf. Ester 3:12; 8:8, 10). Even Jesus, the Son of Man, was sealed by the Father (cf. 6:27). In this vein to be sealed or marked is to belong to the one whose seal or mark is upon us, namely God. (cf. CCC, 1320)

7.   The "when" of Confirmation is not only a question concerning the age of reason (normally considered to be seven (7) years of age).

Two possibilities are raised by the *Catechism* regarding the "when" of the celebration of Confirmation, namely separately from Baptism and during the Eucharist. The first of these seems to presuppose that Confirmation may also be celebrated together with Baptism, as in fact is the case in the East, and with those who are of "catechetical age" (seven or older) in the West, providing us with a third "when." A fourth "when" might even be as a part of a *Liturgy of the Word* or *Liturgy of the Hours*, but these are not specifically mentioned here by the *Catechism*.

For centuries in the West the norm has been for Confirmation to be celebrated separately from Baptism. The scenario plays out like this: once the person who was baptized as an infant reaches the age of reason further sacraments are received, namely: Penance, First Eucharist and Confirmation. More often than not, the first Confession and first Communion are pared together leaving Confirmation seemingly as a stand alone. Confirmation, however, presupposes Baptism.

Before we can be strengthened for Christian living in Confirmation we must be living Christian lives, which begins with grace and faith and Baptism. Regularly and faithfully making a good Confession and worthily receiving Holy Communion helps to keep us faithful to both our Baptism and Confirmation.

When Confirmation is not celebrated together with Baptism it is most often and perhaps best celebrated during the Eucharist. The celebration of Confirmation within the Eucharist highlights the unity of the Sacraments of Christian Initiation: Baptism, Confirmation, and Eucharist. Of these three only the Eucharist is received repeatedly, even daily, but especially on Sundays and other Holy Days of Obligation.

Regardless of when the celebration of Confirmation occurs after Baptism, the renewal of baptismal promises in all the rites of Confirmation, reaffirms the link between Baptism and Confirmation. The baptismal promises are manifold: against the devil, his empty works, his empty promises; for God the Father, God the Son, God the Holy Spirit.

These are promises are made with the aid of God's grace.

These promises can only be kept thanks to God's grace at work in us and our cooperation with God's grace. The graces, of course, linked especially with Baptism are Faith, Hope, and Charity (cf. 1 Corinthians 13:13). While the graces especially linked with Confirmation are seen in the prophetic utterance of Isaiah, namely: Wisdom, Understanding, Counsel, Fortitude, Knowledge, Piety, and Fear of the Lord (cf. Isaiah 11:2-3). These graces are enduring in those who have received these sacraments and may be called upon by the faithful to live holy lives pleasing in the sight of God. (cf. CCC, 1321)

The Lord Jesus Christ, on the night before He died instituted the Sacraments of the Eucharist and Holy Orders, commanding that the Apostles "do this in memory of Me" (cf. Luke 22:19-20; 1 Corinthians 11:24-25;). Some notable features of this image include the Apostle Saint John kneeling to receive Holy Communion from the Lord Himself while Judas who is the only figure depicted without a halo is masked in darkness in the upper left departing the Supper to betray the Lord.

EUCHARIST

1.   "Jesus said: 'I am the living bread, come down from Heaven. Whoever eats this bread will live forever (...). Whoever eats My Flesh and drinks My Blood has eternal life (...) He remains in Me and I in him' (Saint John 6:51, 54, 56)."

The most frequently cited source for the *Catechism of the Catholic Church* is the Holy Bible, Sacred Scripture. Here, when treating the Eucharist this is evident. When considering the Eucharist the Church turns in a special way to the sixth chapter of the Gospel of Saint John, which has been called in part 'the Bread of Life' discourse. This passage from Holy Writ contains a description, a promise and two great mysteries.

In describing the Holy Eucharist, the Lord Jesus speaks of 'Living bread come down from Heaven.' This is both an allusion to the 'manna in the wilderness' and a contrast with it (cf. John 6:31; Exodus 16:4).

Both the Eucharist and the manna are of heavenly origin, but manna was a food which perished as did they who ate it, whereas the Eucharist endures and preserves the souls of them who receive it well (cf. John 6:32; Exodus 16:19-21). The manna is a prefiguration of the Eucharist.

The Lord makes a promise when teaching about the Holy Eucharist: 'Whoever eats this bread will live forever.' The word here translated as 'eats' comes from the Greek word *trogo* which is a verb literally meaning to chew or gnaw. This sort of vocabulary leads to eucharistic realism. When your dog is gnawing or chewing on a bone, there is something real going on there. So too, when we eat the flesh of the Son of Man we are nourished spiritually, by His grace.

One great mystery of the Eucharist is that it enables us to actually eat the Flesh and drink the Blood of the eternal Son of God made man. Throughout the Old Testament there are about 250 references to bread as food and another 175 about drinking wine. It is one thing to have an ordinary meal, breakfast, lunch, dinner. It is something else altogether when what is consumed is God Himself.

When we eat an ordinary meal the food becomes a part of us. When we receive the Eucharist well we become a part of Christ, His Mystical Body, Mother Church, which leads us yet to another mystery.

Another great mystery of the Eucharist is how it is a sacrament of union. Worthy reception of the Eucharist introduces afresh the person who receives and the Lord who is received. Of old it was said of Israel "what nation has God so near" (cf. Deuteronomy 4:7). There is no distance between the one who receives the Eucharist well and the Lord Jesus who is received. (cf. CCC, 1406)

2.   Citing the Dogmatic Constitution on the Church, *Lumen Gentium*, 11, the *Catechism* highlights six (6) important points about the Eucharist for our consideration:

First, the Eucharist is the heart and summit of the life of the Church. The Eucharist is the source of the life of the Church because Christ, the Founder of Mother Church, is present in the Eucharist.

The Eucharist is the summit of the life of the Church because the One we adore and receive in the Eucharist, Christ Himself, is the same who is at the Father's right hand in Heaven.

Second, through the Eucharist Christ associates His Church to His one only sacrifice of the Cross (cf. 1 Peter 3:18). The one only sacrifice of Good Friday is made present throughout the ages each time the Holy Mass is offered. Only the manner of offering is different, now through the ministry of priests, sacramentally, present under the appearances of bread and wine.

Third, through the Eucharist Christ associates all His members to His one only sacrifice of the Cross. Because the one only sacrifice of the Cross is made present through the mystery of the Mass, all of the faithful are able to be present and be united to Christ in His self-offering.

Fourth, Christ's one only sacrifice of the Cross was offered to the Father both in praise and thanksgiving. The Eucharistic Sacrifice continues the praise and thanksgiving which Christ initiated on Good Friday.

In the Eucharistic Sacrifice we praise and thank God who saves and loves us.

Fifth, it is through the Eucharistic Sacrifice that Jesus Christ spreads the graces of salvation. The graces of salvation flow from Jesus' one only sacrifice on the Cross which is made present thorough the mystery of the Mass. The Eucharistic Sacrifice enables us to receive the Lord of Glory as our holy food, His grace and power in our lives, and unites us with Our Lady and Saint John at the foot of the Cross with faith and devotion and love.

Sixth, the Eucharist, the Body of Christ, nourishes the Church, the Body of Christ. The phrase 'Body of Christ' embodies for believers precious doctrine. The Church is the Mystical Body of Christ (cf. Ephesians 5:30). The Eucharist is the Sacramental Body of Christ (cf. John 6:55). Christ Himself was born of Mary in Bethlehem, His body was wrapped in swaddling clothes (cf. Luke 2:7). In His saving Passion, the Body of Christ was nailed to the Cross (cf. John 19:17).

On Easter and in His Ascension Christ rose bodily in triumph and glory not only from the dead but to the Father's right hand in Heaven. All of this and more makes up our Eucharistic Faith, which daily strengthens us for living holy lives. (cf. CCC, 1407)

3.   Four distinct components of the Holy Mass or eucharistic celebration are highlighted as being essential or necessary. Together these form or constitute one single and same act of authentic Christian worship.

The first essential part of Holy Mass is the proclamation of the Word of God. The proclamation of the Word of God includes the reading from Sacred Scripture. Daily readings during the Holy Mass include a passage from one of the Gospels (Matthew, Mark, Luke, or John), a Psalm, and at least one reading either from the Old or New Testament. Holy Mass on Sundays and other great Solemnities and Feasts include one reading from both the Old and New Testament together with a Psalm and Gospel passage.

It should be remembered that all of these various readings from Sacred Scripture refer our attention to Jesus Christ who is the Word made flesh and the fulfillment of the Law and the Prophets (cf. Matthew 5:17; John 1:14).

The second essential part of Holy Mass is the thanksgiving to God the Father for all His good deeds, above all for the gift of His Son. The word "eucharist" comes from the Greek word for thanksgiving, *eucharistesas*. Thanks is given to God for creation, redemption, and His mysterious providence whereby the universe and history are governed. The Incarnation, when God became like us in all things is the apex of creation. The eternal Son made man in Christ Jesus was given us first through the Blessed Virgin Mary and continually is given to us in the Eucharist through Mother Church, through which we become adopted sons and daughters of God. The eucharistic prayer encapsulates all this.

The third essential part of Holy Mass is the consecration of bread and wine.

At the heart of the Eucharistic Prayer can be found the words of consecration spoken by the Bishop or Priest: "...This is My Body..." "...This is My Blood..." Without the consecration there is no transubstantiation, no Mass, no communion...

The fourth essential part of Holy Mass consists in participation in the liturgical banquet by reception of the Body and Blood of the Lord. There are varying degrees of participation which occur during the Holy Mass. Whoever comes with faith and devotion and reverence participates well. Those who come without faith or devotion or reverence participate poorly. Whoever listens attentively to the Word of God participates well. Those who do not attentively follow the readings and prayers participate poorly. Those who are free from mortal sin and have observed the eucharistic fast for at least an hour before Communion and receive the Lord in a state of grace participate well. Those who find themselves in whatever irregular situations (mortal sin...) participate well by abstaining from any sacrilegious reception of Holy Communion. (cf. CCC, 1408)

4.	Four (4) considerations regarding the Eucharist as a memorial

should be considered in order to help us appreciate our Eucharistic

faith.

The Eucharist is the memorial of the Passover of Christ. It was

at the Last Supper (or First Mass) that Jesus said: "Do this in memory

of Me" (cf. Luke 22:19; 1 Corinthians 11:24-25). The Greek word

anamnesis is sometimes translated as "commemoration" or

"recollection" or "remembrance." The Hebrew words *zekher* and

zikkaron are translated as "memorial." The memorial sacrifices go

both ways, bringing the worshiper before God and God to the

worshiper. For Christians there are two (2) major commemorations of

Passover, the Old and the New. To read about the Old Passover we

look at Exodus 12 about the Passing over of the angel of death and the

liberation of the Jewish people from slavery to Pharaoh. When

considering the New Passover we look to Jesus, the "Lamb of God

who takes away the sins of the world" who died once for all (cf. John

1:29; 1 Corinthians 15:3; 2 Corinthians 5:15; 1 Peter 3:18).

The Eucharist is the memorial of the work of salvation. The Eucharist is a continuation of the mighty words and deeds done by Jesus Christ (cf. Luke 24:19; John 6:27-28). The notion of the Greek and Hebrew words (*anamnesis* and *sekher, zikkaron* respectively) makes present the past with a view to the future. Our faith in the Eucharist is faith in Jesus Christ sent by the Father for our salvation (cf. John 6:29). This sending was not only at Nazareth when He was conceived by the power of the Holy Spirit, nor only at Bethlehem where He was born in the fullness of time but at each and every Mass when the bread and wine are changed into Christ Himself, body, blood, soul, and divinity, Christ is present (cf. Matthew 2:1; Luke 1:26; 2:4-7; Galatians 4:4).

The Eucharist memorializes the life, death, and resurrection of Christ. Christ lived a human life like all of us. As each of us will die, unless Christ returns in glory first, Christ Himself died on Good Friday. As Christ rose again from the dead on the first Easter Sunday, so we will rise again on the last day, even though we have already been raised with Him in Baptism (cf. Romans 14:9; Colossians 2:12).

The Eucharist makes present, via the liturgical action, the work of salvation, namely, the life, death and resurrection of Christ. The sacraments have power as conduits of God's grace. The Eucharist all the more so since it is Christ Himself. The liturgical rites themselves also have a power proper to them in making present the redemption wrought by Christ. We have access to Christ's life, death and resurrection through the liturgy. (cf. CCC, 1409)

5. Four considerations help us to further appreciate the mystery of the Eucharist.

First, we consider Christ, the great eternal priest of the New Covenant. Considering Christ's priesthood requires us to also consider the *Letter to the Hebrews*. As high priest, Christ is both merciful and faithful. He has in Himself become a propitiation for our sins, once for all (cf. Hebrews 2:17). Jesus Christ is the apostle and high priest of our confession of faith (cf. Hebrews 3:1). Because our high priest Jesus Christ has passed into the heavens we are to hold fast to our confession of faith (cf. Hebrews 4:14).

62

None should deny Christ's high priesthood (cf. Hebrews 5:10; 6:20; 7:17, 21, 26; 8:1). Considering the New Covenant both implies and presupposes the covenants of old (think of Noah, Abraham, Moses, David...).

Second, we consider that Christ, through the ministry of priests, offers the eucharistic sacrifice. Again, the *Letter to the Hebrews* helps. As Christ Himself was and is a man among men, so too His priests (cf. Hebrews 5:1). Christ offered Himself, once for all on the Cross on Good Friday. Now, the one only sacrifice which was anticipated at the Last Supper is continuously made present through the mystery of the eucharistic sacrifice. Only the manner of offering is changed. It was when the Lord commanded the Apostles (and their successors the bishops and their collaborators the priests) to 'do this in memory of Me' that the New Testament priesthood was established (cf. Luke 22:19; 1 Corinthians 11:24).

A third consideration highlights that Christ Himself is present under the consecrated species of bread and wine.

Two (2) infamous errors which have appeared over the centuries concern Christ's eucharistic presence, namely *inmpanation* and *transsignification*. These heresies, respectively, teach that Christ is in the bread and wine (and that the substance of the bread and wine thereby still remain after the consecration) and that only what is signified by the bread and wine changes (not the substance of the bread and wine). Catholics believe that while the accidents (appearances: sight, smell, taste, weight...) of the bread and wine remain the same before, during and after the consecration, the substance (being, existential reality) changes into Christ Himself.

A fourth eucharistic consideration is that Christ Himself is offered in the eucharistic sacrifice. Not only is the Lord present in the Sacrament of the Altar, but His one only offering is made present throughout the ages until He returns in glory to judge the living and the dead (cf. Acts 10:42; 2 Timothy 4:1; Hebrews 10:10; 1 Peter 4:5). All the acts of Jesus Christ, true God and true man, have eternal ramifications, due to His divine nature. This includes His self-offering both on the Cross and in the Eucharist. (cf. CCC, 1410)

6.   When considering the Sacrament of the Most Holy Eucharist, Mother Church insists on the importance of validly ordained priests. Both the Sacrament of Holy Orders and the Sacrament of the Holy Eucharist were instituted by Jesus Christ at the Last Supper. This is further evidence of their close relationship. While the *Catechism* has an entire section on Holy Orders, which we will treat elsewhere, here further mention is also made of that Sacrament of Service in conjunction with this Sacrament of Initiation.

Validly ordained priests are required for the Eucharist. Without a priest there is no Holy Mass. The enemies of Christ and His Kingdom have known this throughout the ages and when trying to stamp out the Gospel, often do so by persecution of the clergy (consider France 1793-1797 even imprisoning Pope Pius VI; Mexico 1823-1934 with the Martyr Saint Miguel Augustine Pro, S.J. among others; Philippines 1896-1904 with the expulsion or imprisonment of Augustinians, Franciscans and Jesuits alike; Poland 1939-1989 with Martyrs such as Saint Maximilian Marie Kolbe, O.F.M. and Blessed Jerzy Popielusko).

Validly ordained bishops (or priests) preside at the Eucharist. Not only do the priests utter the words of consecration and confect the Sacrament of the Altar, but they also lead the prayers, directing their own attention and that of all present toward God the Father, through the Son, in the Spirit.

Validly ordained bishops (or priests) consecrate the bread and wine during the Eucharist. The one only Sacrifice of Calvary is made present, albeit in an unbloody manner, through the offering of the eucharistic sacrifice, the double apex being the consecration and the communion. While anyone who is in a state of grace, has faith and the use of reason may validly and worthily receive Holy Communion, only bishops and priests are able, by the power of God, to change bread and wine into Christ, whole and entire.

Via the consecration bread and wine become the Body and Blood of the Lord Jesus Christ who commands that this be done in memory of Him (cf. Luke 22:19; 1 Corinthians 11:24). Failing to keep the Lord's memory in this way is to fail Him.

66

Besides a validly ordained bishops (or priests) using the valid words of consecration, also required for a true Eucharist is valid matter, namely bread and wine. Just as there is no Baptism without water and the words 'I baptize you in the Name of the Father, and of the Son, and of Holy Spirit', so bread and wine are necessary prerequisites for the Holy Sacrifice of the Mass. Rice cakes and saki are not valid matter. Beer and pizza likewise are not valid matter. While sacrilegious parodies have been attempted, Christ's sovereign choice here is normative and binding. We celebrate His sacraments His way. (cf. CCC, 1411)

7.   The *Catechism* draws our attention to three (3) important elements when considering the Holy Eucharist: the matter, the form and the working of the Holy Spirit.

Each of the sacraments have specific matter and form. The essential signs or matter of the Eucharist are bread of wheat and wine from the vine. Throughout Sacred Scripture bread is the primary food (cf. Genesis 3:19).

Beaten or bruised, meal, and fine meal are three different sorts of flour

mentioned in Sacred Scripture from which bread, the staple of life, is

made (cf. Genesis 18:6; Exodus 29:2; Leviticus 2:2, 14,16; 6:15).

Wine also is repeatedly mentioned throughout Sacred Scripture,

especially as the product of grapes with intoxicating properties (cf.

Deuteronomy 12:17; 18:4; Judges 9:13; Hosea 4:11; Acts 11:13).

Both the making of bread and of wine require that the grain and the

grapes are not only sifted and cleaned but pounded and ground in the

process, which aptly mirrors what happened to the Lord on Good

Friday when He was bruised for our offenses, crushed for our sins (cf.

Isaiah 53:5-6). The beatings of Good Friday with the death of the Lord

upon the Cross are likewise seen in the kneading and baking required

for the making of bread.

Upon the bread and wine are pronounced the words of

consecration spoken by the Lord Jesus at the Last Supper. The words

of consecration are "this is My Body given up for you. (...) This is the

chalice of My Blood..." (Cf. Matthew 26:17-29; Mark 14:12-25; Luke

22:7-20).

While there does exist a *Eucharistic Prayer* or *Anaphora* attributed to *Addai* and *Mari* (of the Chaldean East Syrian Rite) which is said to be valid even though it omits the specific words of consecration, this prayer is NOT found in the *Roman Missal* of any edition (2000, 1975, 1970., 1962, 1955, 1920, 1884, 1634, 1604, 1570...). The venerable *Roman Canon*, used in an nearly exclusive manner for more than a millennia includes both the invocation of the Holy Spirit (esp. via the gesture) and the words of consecration as integral parts of the rite.

Even before the consecration of the bread and wine, in order that these simple elements be changed entirely into Christ, a special prayer calling forth the Holy Spirit is made. This invocation of the Holy Spirit is called the *epiclesis*. All the sacraments include an *epiclesis* or calling down of the Holy Spirit. The gesture which accompanies the invocation of the Holy Spirit is outstretched hands, which overshadow that upon which the Spirit is called, in the case of the Holy Eucharist, the bread and the wine to be changed into Christ who Himself was conceived by the power of the same Holy Spirit who overshadowed the Blessed Virgin Mary. (cf. CCC, 1412)

8.   Some specific terms are used by Catholics when speaking about the eucharistic reality. Here we consider three of them.

Consecration" occurs at Holy Mass, during the Eucharistic Prayer. The words of consecration are: "this is My body… this is .. My blood…"

The term "transubstantiation" refers to the effect of the consecration of the bread and wine at Holy Mass so that they become Christ whole and entire. Transubstantiation means an underlying change of the substance (being) of the bread and wine into Christ, whole and entire. (There are heretical ways people have spoken about the Eucharist: consubstantiation, transignification, impanation…).

When using the terms "consecrated species" Mother Church refers to what was bread and wine before the consecration, namely bread and wine. What does remain the same before and after the consecration are the weight, shape, taste of bread and wine.

Seven aspects of the phrase "Real Presence" in connection with the Eucharist should be considered:

Christ's body is present in the Eucharist. The same who was born in Bethlehem and who died and was buried and who rose and ascended to Heaven and who will come to judge the living and the dead is present in the Eucharist.

Christ's blood is present in the Eucharist. Part of the reality of the resurrection is that Jesus' body and soul have been reunited (although the Person of the Word remained present to both during the three days in the tomb, and during the Harrowing of Hell, (cf. 1 Peter 3:19).

Christ's soul is present in the Eucharist. Again, because of the reality of the resurrection, because Christ is present in the Eucharist, He is present entirely. If His soul were not present in the Eucharist but His body and blood were… something would be missing.

Christ's divinity is present in the Eucharist. Because Jesus Christ is true God and true man, wherever His human nature is His divine nature also should be, hence in the Eucharist Christ's divinity is also present.

The living Christ is present in the Eucharist, again, reaffirming our Easter faith in the resurrection.

The glorious Christ is present in the Eucharist. Christ who is victorious over sin and death, the Cross and the grave, who is at the Father's right hand in heavenly glory is really present.

Christ is substantially present in the Eucharist. Christ's substantial presence, refers to Jesus' very being, which according to our Trinitarian faith He shares in common with the Father and the Holy Spirit.

The *Catechism* cites the Council of Trent (AD 1545–1563) reminding us that doctrine does not change. Saint Thomas Aquinas (+1274) lived before Trent, what he believed, the Fathers at Trent believed, the Fathers at the two councils at the Vatican (AD 1869–1870, AD 1962–1965) believed, we believe… (cf. CCC, 1413)

9. Consideration of four (4) aspects of the Eucharist as a sacrifice will help us to have a more complete understanding of so great a sacrament. First of all, we should consider that the Eucharist is a sacrifice.

Christ Himself offered Himself up for our redemption on Good Friday, even as He anticipated it on Holy Thursday at the Last Supper, commanding that we do this in memory of Him (cf. Matthew 26:26–28; Mark 14:22–24; Luke 22:15–21; Corinthians 11:25; Hebrews 9:14, 28). When the Lord first said "…My body given for you… My blood, which shall be shed for you" the sacrifice of Good Friday was anticipated. Part of the mystery of the Holy Mass is that it makes present in the here and now what happened both in the Upper Room and on Calvary (cf. Matthew 27:51; Mark 15:37; Luke 23:46; John 19:30).

Second, the Eucharistic sacrifice is offered in reparation for the sins of the living and the dead. The Old Testament knew of "peace offerings"(cf. Leviticus 3:1–17; 6:12; 7:1-) and "sin offerings" (cf. Exodus 29:10-; Leviticus 4:1–35; 6:24–30); and "guilt offering" (cf. Leviticus 5:14–6:7). These sacrifices were but preparations for Christ's one only sacrifice which is perpetuated and made present in the mystery of the Mass. The Roman Canon has two (2) explicit "mementos," one for the living and one for the dead.

This is just one way in which the sacrifice of the Mass is offered in reparation, the priest's intention. Another is by the intention of the faithful present. Yet still another way reparation for sins is made through the Sacrifice of the Mass is through the sacrificial offering (Mass stipend) often made together with the request that the Holy Mass be offered for a particular needy soul.

Third, the Eucharistic sacrifice is offered in order to obtain from God spiritual benefits. Most frequently the Mass is requested so as to obtain from God special graces and virtues and growth in holiness for ourselves, our loved ones, the world.... An example is seen in the Nuptial Mass which is offered not only in thanksgiving for the couple who have found each other and committed themselves to each other, but also to ask for choice blessings from God safeguarding indissoluble unity... These are some spiritual benefits, there are others.

Finally, the Eucharistic sacrifice may also be and often is offered in order to obtain temporal benefits for ourselves and others.

Temporal benefits include, but are not limited to acquiring gainful employment, academic or professional goals and the like. The various professions (e.g. through the "Red Mass," the "White Mass," and the "Blue Mass") call down blessings respectively upon judges and lawyers, doctors and nurses, and the police as each serves the common good of society. (cf. CCC, 1414)

10.   The reception of Holy Communion has certain pre-requisites: we are to be Catholics in full communion with the Church, believing all that She believes; we are to abstain from any ordinary food for an hour before Holy Mass; we are to be well disposed and approach with supernatural motives (not just habit or out of human respect).

To receive Holy Communion well we are to be in a "state of grace" which is to say we are free from mortal sin. We are able to be in a state of grace thanks to God's grace at work in us. After we have received Holy Baptism we are in a state of grace. After a good confession we are in a state of grace.

If we sadly find ourselves in a state of mortal sin, the absolution of mortal sins in the Sacrament of Penance is necessary in order to return to the state of grace so as to worthily receive Holy Communion.

In Sacred Scripture we read: "Whosoever shall eat the Bread, or drink the Chalice of the Lord unworthily, shall be guilty of the Body and the Blood of the Lord" (1 Corinthians 11:27). Saint Paul wrote these inspired words in the first century, and the teaching remains unchanged. Recall that the *Catechism* was published by Blessed John Paul II in 1992. Benedict XVI used the phrase "eucharistic consistency" in *Sacramentum Caritatis*, (22 February, 2007), 83, to make the same point. Jorge Mario Cardinal Bergoglio, Archbishop of Buenos Aires, Argentina and chairman of the editorial committee of the Latin American Bishops Conference (CELAM) (the future Pope Francis) preferred the phrase "eucharistic coherence" in the *Aparecida Document* (29 May, 2007), 436.

For Benedict XVI, eucharistic consistency includes the understanding that our faith and prayer life "can never be a purely private matter" and "it demands a public witness to our faith.... this is true for all the baptized" and especially "those who, by virtue of their social or political position" "make decisions regarding fundamental values" such as "respect for human life, its defense from conception to natural death, the family built upon marriage between a man and a woman, the freedom to educate one's children and the promotion of the common good in all its forms. These values are not negotiable."... For Benedict "There is an objective connection here with the Eucharist (cf. *1 Cor* 11:27-29)."

For the future Pope Francis eucharistic coherence includes being committed to the truth that

> "people cannot receive Holy Communion and at the same time act or speak against the commandments, in particular when abortion, euthanasia, and other serious crimes against life and family are facilitated. This responsibility applies particularly to legislators, governors, and health professionals."[5]

May we always be faithful to the Eucharistic Christ. (cf. CCC, 1415)

11.   One who receives Holy Communion is called a "communicant." "Daily communicants" are those who come to Holy Mass each day, not just on Sundays and other Holy Days of Obligation, participating devoutly, including not only reception of the Word of God in Sacred Scripture but also the Word made flesh, Christ in the Eucharist.

---

[5]

cf. *Aparecida*, (2007) 436. Pope Francis has cited the *Aparecida* document repeatedly in his pontificate, i.e. "Carta a la 105 Conferencia Episcopal Argentina (25 Marzo, 2013); *Evangelii Gaudium* (24 November, 2013) 124, notes 4, 17, 21, 63, 98, 103, 106, 147; *Laudato si* (24 May, 2015) 54, notes 24, 32.

Five specific graces are recognized by Mother Church as being especially linked to our worthy reception of Holy Communion.

The first specific grace resulting from a worthy reception of Holy Communion is union with the Lord Jesus whom we receive sacramentally, Body, Blood, Soul and Divinity. What we long to experience in Heaven, eternal union, is anticipated here below through the Sacrament of the Altar. How much closer could we get to God or God to us? When we eat ordinary food it becomes a part of us, we assimilate it. When we receive the Eucharist well, however, we are the ones who are assimilated, taken up into Christ and His Mystical body the Church.

A second specific grace flowing from the worthy reception of Holy Communion is the reinforced ties of charity with Christ. God who is love (charity) becomes our food in Holy Communion (cf. John 6:51-56; 1 John 4:8).

Even before the French gastronomist Anthelme Brillat-Savarin wrote in 1826 words to the effect that "you are what you eat" faithful followers of the Lord Jesus had known this for centuries as witnessed by Patristic and Scholastic Theology (Saint Justin Martyr, *Apology*, 66; Saint Cyprian, *On the Sacrament of the Cup of the Lord*, 13; Saint Thomas Aquinas, *Summa Theologiae* III, Q. 74, 6-8).

A third specific grace which is a consequence of receiving Holy Communion well is the remission of venial sins. Forgiveness of mortal sins requires sacramental Confession with absolution. The reception of Holy Communion is one of several sanctioned means of receiving God's mercy for venial sins (others include the devout use Holy Water making the Sign of the Cross, devout reading from Sacred Scripture for more than thirty (30) minutes, praying the Holy Rosary aloud with others in Church; cf. CCC §§ 1471-1479; *Manual of Indulgences* [2012]).

A fourth specific grace available to us through our worthy reception of Holy Communion is preservation from grave sins.

This is so because of the powerful graces given in the Eucharist as well as a motivation for not sinning mortally, which would hinder any further reception of Holy Communion until making a good Confession.

Finally, a fifth specific grace resulting from Holy Communion well received is our reinforced unity with the Church, the Mystical Body of Christ. The Church is made up of many members, some already in Heaven others still on Earth and yet others undergoing final purification (cf. Romans 12:4). (cf. CCC, 1416)

12. As followers of the Lord Jesus Christ, we have both the obligation and the privilege of receiving Holy Communion at least once each year (annually). This reception has been called our "Easter duty." The Easter Duty is spelled out for us elsewhere: *"... humbly receive your Creator in Holy Communion at least during the Easter season, guarantees as a minimum the reception of the Lord's Body and Blood in connection with the Paschal feasts, the origin and center of the Christian liturgy"* (*Catechism* § 2042).

Mother Church has repeated this bare minimum repeatedly, at the Synod of Agde (508AD), Lateran IV (1215 AD), and most famously during Trent (1545-1563 AD; session XIII, Canon ix). The *1983 Code of Canon Law,* canon 920 §§1-2 addresses it this way: *"After being initiated into the Most Holy Eucharist, each of the faithful is obliged to receive Holy Communion at least once a year; this precept must be fulfilled during the Easter season unless it is fulfilled for a just cause at another time during the year."* The time frame for the Easter Duty is rendered variously as "Paschal Tide" or "Easter Season," from the Vigil of Easter through second Vespers of the Ascension or Pentecost.

Just because we are obliged to receive Holy Communion, as a minimum, during the Easter Time, is not to disregard the obligation we have to participate in the Sunday Mass (or Saturday Vigil for Sunday) each week, affording us the opportunity to receive Holy Communion weekly (cf. *Catechism of the Catholic Church* § 2042).

The daily reception of Holy Communion should also be considered.

In the *Lord's Prayer* we ask the Lord to "give us this day our daily bread" referring not only to breakfast, lunch, and dinner, but also to the bread come down from Heaven which is the Holy Eucharist (cf. Luke 11:3). In the first century, the Apostolic Church enjoyed the practice of gathering daily in the Temple for readings from Sacred Scripture as well as the "breaking of bread," another way of speaking of the Eucharist (cf. Acts 2:46).

We are to participate in the Eucharistic Celebration at least each Sunday and other Holy Days of Obligation. Full, active, conscious participation, includes: not only timely presence (late arrival and early departure without a serious reason is sacrilegious, disrespecting the Lord and the faithful who actually wish to give Him His due), standing, sitting, kneeling, making appropriate responses at the appropriate time(s), listening attentively to the Sacred Scriptures proclaimed, together with the worthy reception of Holy Communion rounds out our worshipful experience.

Mother Church does recommend with lively concern our frequent, even daily reception of Eucharistic Holy Communion, so does the Lord Jesus Himself: "...take this... do this... in memory of Me" (cf. Matthew 26:26-28; Mark 14:22-24; Luke 22:15-20; 1 Corinthians 11:23-29). (cf. CCC, 1417)

13.   Blessed John Paul II in his *Catechism* cites one of his predecessors, Paul VI, who wrote about the Holy Eucharist in his encyclical letter *Mysterium Fidei*, (3 September, 1965). Five (5) things stand out here.

First, Christ the Lord is present in the Sacrament of the Altar, this is 'Eucharistic Realism." Jesus Christ is true God and true man who with the Eternal Father holds all of creation in existence. Jesus Christ waited for some nine (9) months hidden in the maternal tabernacle which was Our Lady's immaculate womb (cf. Luke 1:26-2:14).

He who had the power to change water into wine, has the power to change bread and wine into His very self, to become our 'daily bread' (cf.. Luke 22:15-19; John 2:1-11; 6:51-56; 1 Corinthians 11:23-25...).

Second, Christ the Lord, present in the Sacrament of the Altar must be honored with a cult of adoration. "Eucharistic Realism" requires that Christ Jesus who is true God and true man, who changes bread and wine into His very self, to become our holy food, is worthy of worship. The phrase 'cult of adoration' is technical and at the heart of our faith. The word 'adore' derives from the Latin *adorare*, having at least five (5) meanings: to speak to, to beseech, to entreat, to do homage, to worship. The Latin *cultus* refers to a specific form of worship. The worship (*latria*) given to Christ present in the Blessed Sacrament of the Altar, the Holy Eucharist is the same as that which is rightfully directed toward the Father and the Holy Spirit, God the Holy Trinity. Exposition, adoration and benediction of the Blessed Sacrament embody a classic form of wholesome Eucharistic Piety.

(*Hyperdulia* and *douleia*, the honor, devotion, veneration and respect shown to the Virgin Mary and to the other saints and holy angels respectively is different altogether.)

Third, to visit Christ the Lord in the Most Holy Sacrament of the Altar is a proof of gratitude. When we visit Christ in the tabernacle we come with grateful hearts, thanking Him for the various blessings of the day.

Fourth, to visit Christ the Lord in the Most Holy Sacrament of the Altar is a sign of love. We show our love for Him who laid down His life for love of us by visiting Christ who awaits our visit so as to shower us with His love from the tabernacle.

Finally, to visit Christ the Lord in the Most Holy Sacrament of the Altar is a Christian duty. Even apart from the solemn exposition, adoration and benediction of the Blessed Sacrament in the monstrance, Christ the Lord waits in the tabernacle for us to come visit Him.

Church buildings are open some hours each day to allow our pious visits. (cf. CCC, 1418)

86

14.   Saint Thomas Aquinas' prayer *O Sacrum Convivium* finds it's way not only as the *Magnificat Antiphon* of Second Vespers of *Corpus Christi*, but also in the Constitution on the Sacred Liturgy, *Sacrosanctum Concilium*, 47, of the Second Vatican Council, as well as here in the *Catechism* at least by allusion. It is good to consider it anew, in four (4) parts.

First, the Eucharistic banquet is a pledge of glory. The Lord Jesus is the Lord of glory and He is present in the Eucharist (cf. 1 Corinthians 2:8; 2 Corinthians 3:18-19; 2 Thessalonians 1:9; 2:14; Jude 1:24). The Hebrew term *yah-yin* and the Greek term *dokh-ay* are often translated as either banquet or feast (cf. Song of Songs 2:4; Esther 7:2; Luke 5:29; 14:12-24). The Eucharist is all the more so both banquet and feast in which that which is eaten is God Himself.

Second, our participation in the Holy Eucharistic Sacrifice of the Mass identifies us with the Sacred Heart of Jesus.

The Hebrew term *lebh* and the Greek term *kardia* refer not only to the physiological organ which pumps blood throughout the living being, but also the emotions such as anger, courage, fear, hatred, joy, love, sorrow and the like as well as the person (cf. Deuteronomy 19:6; Psalm 4:7; 13:2; 27:14; 1 Samuel 25:37...). Of course, in Christ Jesus, true God and true man, these are all perfectly ordered. In the case of the Sacred Heart of Jesus, the Second Person of the Most Holy Trinity is not only represented but He feeds us with His very self in Holy Communion. We gaze upon the Sacred Host lifted high above the altar remembering the blood and water which flowed from Christ's pierced side as we adore and receive the living, glorious, risen Lord as our holy food which makes us His holy people when well received (cf. John 19:33-37).

Third, the Eucharist gives us strength for the pilgrimage of our life to Heaven. The Prophet Elias was strengthened by God's food for the journey (cf. 1 Kings 19:4-8).

When we well receive Holy Communion we too are strengthened for the journey of faith lived out day by day until the Lord calls us to render an account or He returns in glory (cf. Matthew 12:36; John 5:22, 30; 8:16; Acts 10:42; 17:31; Romans 2:16; 14:12; 2 Timothy 4:1; James 5:9; 1 Peter 4:5; Hebrews 10:30).

Finally, the Eucharist unites us to the Church in Heaven, with the Holy Virgin Mary and all the Saints. This is because when we receive Holy Communion, the Lord Jesus whom we receive is the same Lord Jesus who is now at the Father's right hand on high, adored by all of the Saints, together with the Blessed Virgin Mary. (cf. CCC, 1419)

Before the Lord Jesus extended His authority to forgive sins to the

Apostles, He forgave many (cf. Matthew 16:19; 18:18; Mark 2:5-9;

Luke 5:20; John 20:23). The adulteress woman came to Him with

great sorrow and great love, she left with peace of heart (cf. Luke 7:37-

50). The Lord exhorts us to sin no more (cf. John 8:11).

PENANCE

1.   On Easter night, the risen Lord Jesus showed Himself to His apostles, breathing upon them saying: 'Receive the Holy Spirit. Whose sins you shall forgive, they are forgiven them: and whose sins you shall retain, they are retained' (cf. John 20:22-23). This passage from Sacred Scripture is not unrelated to Matthew 16:19 where the Lord Jesus gives to Saint Peter (and his successors...) authority to bind and to loose in Heaven and on Earth. Elsewhere we are encouraged by Almighty God to confess our sins, one to another and to pray for each other that we may be saved (cf. James 5:16).

The successors of the apostles are the bishops. The successor of Saint Peter is the Bishop of Rome, the Pope. Because the bishops and the pope are not able to absolve all who need to receive the mercy of God, they have collaborators in the priests who are bound to not reveal anything learned in Confession.

The Greek word *homologeo* and the Hebrew word *yadhah* are translated into English as "confession" meaning acknowledgment, avowal, with the implication of a change of conviction or of course of conduct, placing one in harmony with others. This is not to discount the work of God's grace in both moving us to sorrow for our sins and restoring the harmony.

Many non-Catholics object to the Sacrament of Penance, saying "I go straight to God. I don't confess to a man."

This seems to throw out the very words of the God-man Christ Jesus who gave the apostles (and their successors the bishops and their collaborators the priests) real authority to bind and to loose, to forgive or to retain sins (cf. John 20:22-23).

While Saint James' exhortation does not specifically name priests or restrict confession of sins to priests only, priests being bound by the "seal of Confession" whereby they are bound to NOT reveal what they have learned in the "internal forum" in the "external forum" is a safeguard which allows for both the granting of the absolution and the security of one's reputation.

Priests themselves also need to go to Confession when they find themselves in a state of serious, mortal, grave, sin. All are in need of God's great mercy (cf. Romans 3:23; 5:12). Blessed John Paul II is said to have gone to Confession each week, not necessarily because he was a proverbial 'ax murderer, drug pusher, or pimp' but because he knew and sought to live the *Lord's Prayer* "... forgive us our trespasses..." The Sacrament of Penance is a privileged way wherein Almighty God, through the ministry of His priests grants us mercy, pardon and peace, for those sins we sadly commit after Baptism. (cf. CCC, 1485)

2.   God begins His saving work in us through the saving grace given in Baptism There is a special sacrament, instituted by Christ, which restores us to the life of grace sadly forfeited by post-baptismal sin(s), namely the Sacrament of Penance. Here we consider the four (4) different names for the Sacrament of Penance, each of which highlight a particular aspect of the sacrament.

The Sacrament of Penance is also called the Sacrament of Conversion. Conversion is not only a one time reality. "Once saved, always saved" is foreign to our Catholic way of thinking. Our life in Christ concerns not only our beginning, how we start, but also how we end. The ongoing conversion experienced and exercised in the Sacrament of Penance provides further graces along the way, allowing for correction of course *en route* to Heaven.

The Sacrament of Penance is also called the Sacrament of Confession because we actually tell the priest (or bishop) our sins.

In the Sacrament of Penance we admit our shortcomings, failings and sins, not in a masochistic way, but to allow the healing grace of the Divine Physician to heal and salve us. When we confess our sins in the Sacrament of Penance we say: when our previous confession was (day, week, month...), what our state of life is (single, married, ordained, consecrated...) and identify our sins according to number and kind (e.g. I robed three banks, I told two lies...). This information helps the priest Confessor to help the penitent to grow in the life of grace.

The Sacrament of Penance takes it's name from the assignment given by the priest Confessor as a form of reparation for the sins committed. Sometimes the penance assigned is further prayer (a Hail Mary, Our Father, Glory be, a decade of the Rosary, five mysteries of the Rosary, a week or month of rosaries...). Sometimes the making of a pilgrimage or lighting of votive candle(s) are assigned as a penance. Fasting has also been a classic penance.

The Sacrament of Penance is also known as the Sacrament of Reconciliation. There are four (4) different reconciliations which take place in the Sacrament of Penance: with God, with the Church, with self, with others. When we sin we put distance between ourselves and God's will for our salvation. Mortal sins separate us from the love of God and bar us from reception of Holy Communion. Having received the Sacrament of Penance allows us to return to full communion with Christ, His Church, His sacraments. Sadly, when we sin we prefer creation to the Creator and even ourselves. The Sacrament of Penance restores the proper relationship between ourselves and others, including Almighty God. (cf. CCC, 1486)

3.   There are five different aspects we should consider in relation to the harm sin causes. How often have we heard "I'm not hurting anyone"? We should never forget that the sufferings endured on Good Friday by the Innocent Jesus Christ were directly in proportion to our sins. Sin wounds the honor of God.

God has made us for Himself, and when we sin we disregard His will for us, namely holiness and happiness in both this life and the life to come. The English Martyr Saint Thomas Becket (+1170) did what he did (defending the rights of the Church against encroachment of King Henry II) and suffered what he did (exile and death) all for the honor of God. The ancient Latin hymn by Theodulph of Orleans (+820) *Gloria, laus, et honor* is sung in English as *All glory, laud and honor*, translated by John M. Neale (+1866). Sins are sour notes. Our repentance and confession allow for harmony to be restored.

Sin wounds the love of God. Whenever we sin we prefer or love what is not God or His holy will for us. We prefer the creature to the Creator, spurning the love of God.

Sin wounds the proper human dignity of one called to be an adopted child of God. Sin is an abuse of free will. Being made in the image of God, *imago Dei*, we are called to exercise our freedom well. To say "no one can tell me what to do" may be a sign of a misunderstanding of human freedom, autonomy.

98

Not only can God tell us what good we should do and what evil we should avoid, He has, and continues to do so through His bride and mystical body Mother Church.

Sin wounds the spiritual well being of the Church. One moniker for Mother Church is the 'communion of saints,' *communio sanctorum*. Our sins disfigure the holiness of the Church, while our repentance and graced living are her splendor. Saint John the Evangelist helps us in this regard, when, inspired by the Holy Spirit he wrote: "If we say we are without sin, the truth is not within us" and that the Lord Jesus is "the way, the truth, and the life" (cf. 1 John 1:8; John 14:6). In the Sacrament of Penance we confess our sins, and He who is faithful and just forgives us and purifies us from all unrighteousness (cf. 1 John 1:9).

Mortal (deadly) sin thwarts our being living stones, building up Mother Church. Yet, God's grace, given anew in the Sacrament of Penance, gives us new life in Christ if and whenever we should find ourselves displeasing to God due to our sins. (cf. CCC, 1487)

4.   The eyes of faith recognize sin as the worst of evils. Sacred Scripture relates the life of grace to the ability to see and life lived in sin as blindness (cf. Matthew 13:15-16; 18:9; 20:33-34; Mark 9:47; Luke 10:23; 19:42). There are all sorts of evil things in this world, sufferings, illnesses, death, poverty and the like. Some of these are caused by sin (when I rob you, you suffer; when I beat you up, you suffer; sometimes people die following a physical attack; others contract certain ailments of body (sclerosis of the liver and lung cancer come to mind) as a consequence of the their behavior (excessive drinking and smoking), sloth and greed are often combined in cases of poverty. Sin, however is the worst of evils because sin is an offense against God, "who is all good and worthy of all our love" (*Act of Contrition*). Sins are acts of injustice to God, disregarding His holy will for our salvation, sanctification.

The eyes of faith recognize three who are harmed by every sin, namely the sinner, the Church, the world. How are sinners hurt by sin?

Sinners are hurt by sin, especially if they die in mortal sin, because of the punishment(s) due to sin, temporal punishments in the here and now, eternal punishments for those who die without repentance. The Sacrament of Penance is a privileged moment of repentance, accompanied by the absolution, which gives blessed assurance of God's mercy upon us.

How is the Church hurt by sin? Because the Church is the "communion of saints," when we live wicked, sinful lives, we disfigure the pure, spotless bride of Christ which is Mother Church. The message, the preaching of the Gospel is hindered when believers are steeped in sin. Sadly, it is often said "You talk a good talk, but don't practice what you preach..."? The remedy, of course, is God's grace and the graced living which is the consequence. God raises up saints in every age to answer the problems of the day. We all are called to be those who let God's grace shine, radiating through our holy lives.

How is the world hurt by sin? Recall the fire and brimstone which rained down in the time of Abraham and Lot, due to the sins of two cities (cf. Genesis 19:1-27; Luke 17:29). And if the entire world is wicked, attempting to "normalize" or "mainstream" various sinful behaviors (think of wholesale no-fault divorce and remarriage, sodomistic unions parodying Marriage, abortion on demand, ...) Why should the Lord stay His hand? The time for mercy is now. The only sins which can not and will not be forgiven are those which go unrepented, which go unconfessed. (cf. CCC, 1488)

5.   The Sacrament of Penance allows us to return to communion with God. Because of our wicked sins, communion needs to be restored between us and God. While we sadly have the ability to rupture our communion with God by our sins, abusing our freewill, we are unable on our own to return to communion with God. While Repentance on our part is important and essential for communion with God, it is His initiative which reestablishes us to a state of grace.

102

Returning to communion with God is a movement born of the grace of God. Redemption, repentance, conversion all require God's grace at work in us. We have in the sacraments sure access to the grace of God. Baptismal grace is foundational for our life in Christ. Our sins wound our relationship with God. Mortal sins rupture our communion with God. Whenever we reject sin and Satan and the glamour of evil it is thanks in no small part to God's grace at work in us. God's grace is always radiating out from His throne of mercy. Our acceptance of His grace is itself yet another grace, that His power might be upon us. We receive many specific graces in the Sacrament of Penance, including the restoration to communion with God and return to the state of grace.

The Sacrament of Penance is part of God's mercy and concern for our salvation. While the unrepentant seem content to die in their sins, God wills not the death of the sinner, but that we be converted and live and move and have our being in Him (cf. Ezekiel 18:23; Acts 17:28).

As followers of Jesus Christ we should not persist in a state of sin and the consequent separation from God.

We should ask in prayer to God for the grace of mercy and salvation for both ourselves and for others. Every time we come to the Holy Mass we ask for God's mercy in the Greek *Kyrie Eleison* (Lord Have Mercy) or the Latin *Confiteor* (I confess), for ourselves. It is no less salutary and praiseworthy to ask for God's grace for everyone else as well. Just as we should not limit our lives of prayer to Sunday Mass, so too our prayers of contrition and repentance should not be limited to the *Penitential Rite* of Mass or the Sacrament of Penance, privileged moments though these are. Two helpful prayers are: the "Jesus Prayer" *Lord Jesus Christ, Son of God, have mercy on me, a sinner*"; and the "Fatima Prayer"

> *O my Jesus, forgive us our sins. Save us from the fires of Hell, lead all souls to Heaven especially those in most need of Thy mercy.* (cf. CCC, 1489)

6.   Six important aspects of the Sacrament of Penance which are especially worthy of our consideration. The first aspect to consider is conversion. Without the grace of God there is no conversion. We can and should dispose ourselves to receive the grace of God. We should likewise pray for others to be open to and to receive God's grace, especially the grace of conversion, which is a turning away from sin and a turning toward God.

A second aspect of the Sacrament of Penance which we should consider is repentance. In the Gospels, the Lord Jesus constantly calls us to repentance (cf. Matthew 21:32; Mark 1:15; Luke 17:4). Several words used in Sacred Scripture are at the root of our English word "repent." The Hebrew word *naham* implies difficulty in breathing, as in to groan, sigh, pant, as occurs with lament and grieving. Another Hebrew word, *shubh,* expresses the idea of genuine repentance and expresses the idea of a radical change in our attitude toward sin and God (cf. Deuteronomy 4:30; Nehemiah 1:9; Psalm 7:12; Jeremiah 3:14).

The Greek word *metaneo* signifies turning or changing of mind and opinion with regard to sin (e.g. Matthew 3:2; Mark 1:15; Acts 2:38). The Greek word *metamelomai* signifies the regret, concern and care (e.g. Matthew 21:29, 32; 27:3).

A third consideration when thinking about the Sacrament of Penance is sorrow for sins committed (contrition). It is common to identify two sorts of sorrow: perfect and imperfect contrition. Perfect contrition is motivated by the pure love for God whom we have offended by our sin(s). Imperfect contrition is motivated by the noble desire to not suffer eternally in Hell as a sad consequence of unrepented, unconfessed mortal sins. God does not will the death of the sinner, but that we be converted and live (cf. Ezekiel 18:23), so imperfect contrition is only imperfect in us, since there is no imperfection in God.

Fourthly, aversion for sins committed is a significant aspect of the Sacrament of Penance.

We should have a strong dislike and disinclination for sin based not only on the sad and eternal consequences of unrepented sin(s), but also because they disfigure us and our neighbors.

As the *Act of Contrition* reminds us, a firm purpose to sin no more, is also a major part of the Sacrament of Penance. Sacramental Penance rejects sin, even as our sins reject God. God's grace helps make this purpose firm.

Finally, the past, present and future are all tied together in the Sacrament of Penance. In the here and now we repent past sins committed in view of receiving grace here and now and life on high forever in the next life. (cf. CCC, 1490)

7.   There are four distinct acts or moments which should be considered integral to the Sacrament of Penance, three on the part of the penitent and one on the part of the priest.

The first act of a penitent is repentance. This first act presupposes an examination of conscience.

We are to examine our conscience before the Cross, with the aid of Sacred Scripture (e.g. Romans 1:28-32; 1 Corinthians 5:11; 9-10; Galatians 5:19-21; Ephesians 5:3-5; Colossians 3:5-8; 1 Timothy 9-10; 2 Timothy 2-5; Hebrews 12:16) and the sure and certain teachings of Mother Church. Upon realizing our sins and shortcomings we are able to come to a real sense of sorrow for our sins. When this sorrow is motivated by the pure love of God it is called "perfect contrition." When the sorrow for sins is motivated by a desire to not suffer eternal damnation in Hell it is called "imperfect contrition."

The second act of a penitent is the actual confession or manifestation of sins to the priest-confessor with the firm purpose to accomplish reparation. Having become sorry for our sins we actually present ourselves and our sins to Christ through the ministry of the priests. Admitting our sins and our responsibility for offending God and neighbor. A very wise priest once advised his penitents: "be brief, be blunt, be gone." Regarding the brief-ness, Confession is not counseling.

Regarding blunt-ness we are not to be shy or embarrassed, priests have heard all sorts of things. Regarding gone-ness, go do your penance.

The third and final act of the penitent in the Sacrament of Penance is doing the actual works of reparation. The priest-confessor assigns the penitent a statutory penance, the completion of which is no less integral to the sacrament. These works of reparation often include prayers, pilgrimages, fasting, corporal works of mercy and the like.

The primary act of the priest-confessor is the granting of the absolution to the penitent. The prayer of absolution is an effective utterance. When the police officer says "you are under arrest" or the judge says "you are free to go" it is so. When the priest utters the words of absolution the penitent is absolved, that is, washed and cleansed of the sins well repented and confessed.

The prayer of absolutions is as follows:

> *"God the Father of mercies, through the death and resurrection of His Son, has reconciled the world to Himself, and sent the Holy Spirit among us for the forgiveness of sins. Through the ministry of the Church, may God give you pardon and peace. And I absolve you from your sins, in the Name of the Father, and of the Son, and of the Holy Spirit."*

(cf. CCC, 1491)

8.   Repentance or contrition inspired by motives relevant to the faith, as one of the three acts of the penitent, is a major part of the Sacrament of Penance. There are at least three different psychological elements to repentance: the intellectual, the emotional, and the volitional. It is one thing for us to recognize that we have sinned and that sin is evil, it is another thing for us to be sorry for our sins, and still yet another to want to avoid sin (and it's near occasion) in the future. True repentance is not superficial, but rather goes to the very depth of one's being.

110

The intellectual aspect flows from our very nature as rational animals

from whom God expects reasonable service (cf. Romans 12:1; *logikos*

latreia in Saint Paul's Greek; *rationabile obsequium* in Saint Jerome's

Latin).

Perfect Contrition is motivated by love of Charity towards God

who is love. This is the most relevant motive of faith which we can

have for sorrow for sin. God is love (cf. 1 John 4:8). When we fail to

love the Lord who is love with all our heart, soul and mind, we sin (cf.

Matthew 22:37; Mark 12:30; Luke 10:27). After admitting our sins in

the Sacrament of Penance the penitent actually prays a prayer which is

called a "perfect Act of Contrition" which is as follows:

> *My God, I am sorry for my sins with all my heart. In choosing*
> *to do wrong and failing to do good, I have sinned against You*
> *whom I should love above all. I firmly intend, with Your help,*
> *to do penance, to sin no more, and to avoid whatever leads me*
> *to sin. Our Savior Jesus Christ, suffered and died for us. In*
> *His Name, my God, have mercy. Amen.*

Imperfect Contrition is motivated by other motives.

One motive which is relevant to the faith but not sorrow for sin because of the love of God is to not want to go to Hell, to suffer eternally in hellfire, with eternal separation from God, the torments of devils and other damned souls. Both Dante's *Inferno* and *Saint Patrick's Purgatory* depict sufferings in the next life, which while motivated by reasons of faith, no doubt, are more self-centered than based upon the supernatural love of charity which is required for perfect contrition.

God is God, and while He prefers perfect contrition, He is willing to work with us who fail to meet that mark. In point of fact, imperfect contrition is only imperfect in us. For God desires not the death of the sinner, but that we be converted and live, and there is nothing imperfect in God (cf. Ezekiel 33:11). (cf. CCC, 1492)

9.	The confession of grave sins to a Priest is necessary for anyone who wants to obtain reconciliation with God and with the Church.

All grave sins must be confessed. What makes a sin grave? The Ten Commandments help us to recognize what is grave matter (cf. CCC, 1858). Sometimes these sins are also called "serious" or "mortal." The obvious connection between "grave" and "mortal" is that when one dies (mortality established) then one is buried (in a grave). To risk either grave or mortal sin is "serious" especially in that we have but one life to live. There are three criteria which must be met together in order for a sin to be grave or mortal or serious: that the matter is grave, serious or mortal; that the person knows the gravity or seriousness of the matter; that the person does the serious or grave deed, desire, omission... without any coercion, that is to say, of one's own free will.

The conscience is to be examined carefully. We well examine our conscience before the Cross because Jesus Christ was nailed to the wood of the Cross to save us from ourselves, from our sins. To look upon Christ Crucified helps us to focus on our specific responsibility for His Passion.

Our consciences should also be examined in light of the teachings found throughout Sacred Scripture. While the whole of Sacred Scripture should be considered, just to look at the following five passages allows God's direct help in forming our consciences concerning the evils of: adultery, ambition, coarse joking, debauchery, discord, dissension, drunkenness, envy, factions, fits of rage, foolish talk, greed, hatred, idolatry, impurity, jealousy, magic arts, obscenity, omission of feeding the hungry - giving drink to the thirsty - welcoming the stranger - clothing the naked - visiting the sick and imprisoned, practices of falsehood, selfish ambition, sexual immorality (including fornication, homosexual offenses, and orgies), slanderers, swindling, theft, witchcraft (cf. 1 Corinthians 6:9-10; Galatians 5:19-21; Ephesians 5:3-6; Revelation 22:12-16; Matthew 25:41-46).

One fourth of the *Catechism* is dedicated to treating our moral life in Christ, with particular attention to the Ten Commandments of God, with all their parts. This will all be treated latter.

114

The confession of venial sins, while not necessary in itself, is heartily recommended by Mother Church. If one or two of the three criteria for a mortal sin are missing, then our sins may be venial. In our desire to be the Saints God calls us to be we should even despise our venial sins. Sacramental Confession allows us to renounce our sins and gives the graces needed to overcome and avoid sin in the future. Saint John Vianney and Blessed John Paul II, pray for us! (cf. CCC, 1493)

10.   When considering the Sacrament of Penance, after considering God who is offended by our sins and whose mercy is given to us so as to begin anew, we should consider both the confessor and the penitent. The priest who hears our confession (and gives the absolution) is called "the confessor" while the person confessing is called "the penitent." When priests go to confession, the priest who is confessing is a penitent as well.

The penitents are those who are sorry for their sins and are seeking to receive God's steadfast mercy in the Sacrament of Penance. Penitents are penitents because of the penances they do and the penitential spirit with which they do them.

Upon hearing the confession of the penitent, the confessor proposes certain acts of 'satisfaction' or of 'penance' to the penitent. This is like 'spiritual homework.' Sometimes the penances proposed are prayers (e.g. *Our Father, Hail Mary, Memorare, Rosary...*). Sometimes the penances proposed are mortifications (e.g. fast, abstain from certain food(s) or drink(s) or sweets...). Works of mercy might be proposed as a penance (e.g. feed the hungry, clothe the naked, visit the sick or imprisoned...). The history of the Church demonstrates how the various penances which should be proposed is a very serious manner, as evidenced by the various *Penitentials* drawn up over the years to help confessors propose appropriate penances.

Four major *Penitentials* have been attributed variously to: Saint Finnian (470-550), Saint Columban (543-615), Cummean (circa 650), and Theodore (602-690). The repeated recitation of Psalm 119:1-176 while kneeling, holding the arms outstretched is one of the more impressive penances. Saint Raymond of Penafort (1175-1275) wrote the *Summa Casuum*, one of the most famous *Penitentials* to ever have been written (though it still has not (yet) been translated into English).

The reason why the various penances are proposed is so as to repair the damage caused by our sin(s). There is, in fact, nothing we can do to earn or deserve the mercy, love, or forgiveness of God. "Ask and you shall receive" (cf. John 16:24; Matthew 21:22; Mark 11:24). The Sacrament of Penance is a privileged way of both asking and receiving God's love, mercy, and forgiveness.

By completing the proposed penance we show both the depths of our sorrow for our sins as well as our gratefulness for the new beginning. Completion of the proposed penance also helps to reestablish the proper habits of a disciple of Christ.

We are supposed to be a people of prayer, a people of virtue.

The more we pray and practice the virtues the less room there is for sin

and Satan in our lives. May God's grace abound in us always. (cf.

CCC, 1494)

11.   The grace won by Jesus' death and resurrection are applied to

us in the sacraments which impart His grace and make us holy. For

the renewal of the innocence first given us in Holy Baptism the Lord

Jesus has provided the Sacrament of Penance. Integral to the

Sacrament of Penance is the priest who serves as "the confessor." The

Church's teaching about the confessor's role is very clear. Only priests

may absolve repentant sinners (cf. *CIC '83* canon 965). Bishops,

before they receive the fullness of Holy Orders have already been

ordained priests. Deacons or religious (Sisters, Brothers, Nuns,

Monks) while they may and should pray for our continued conversion

(and their own) are not able to grant the sacramental absolution proper

to the Sacrament of Penance.

The validity of the Sacrament of Penance requires a validly ordained priest to absolve and a repentant sinner who has confessed.

When priests go to confession they too have to go to another priest.

Only priests with faculties may absolve repentant sinners (*cf. CIC '83* canon 966§1). The faculty to grant absolution presupposes priestly ordination and doctrinal soundness (cf. *CIC '83* canon 970). The faculties to absolve are granted (or not) by the local bishop (cf. *CIC '83* canon 969 § 1). When I was ordained a deacon I received faculties to solemnly baptize, to solemnize Marriages, and to preach. Further faculties were given to me when I was ordained a priest, including those to grant absolution to repentant sinners. Because I have faculties to absolve repentant sinners in the Diocese of Knoxville, I likewise have faculties to absolve repentant sinners anywhere, unless the local ordinary (normally a bishop) denies this in a particular case (cf. *CIC '83* canon 967 § 2).

Priests with faculties absolve repentant sinners in the Name and Person of Christ the Head of the Church.

To act in the Name and Person of Christ the Head is the prerogative of the Priest not only at the Altar when consecrating the sacred elements with the words of institution: *This is My Body... this is My Blood...* but also in granting absolution in the Sacrament of Penance: *...I absolve you...* While we may see the priest or hear his voice it is Christ the great High Priest (*Episcopum animarum vestrarum*) who absolves us through the priest and not without the priest (cf. 1 Peter 2:25; The Greek word *episkopos* here translated by Saint Jerome's Latin means superintendent, Christian officer in charge or bishop).

Eeven a priest who lacks the faculty to hear confessions absolves validly and licitly any penitent who is in danger of death from any censures and sins (cf. *CIC '83* canon 976). (cf. CCC, 1495)

12.   There are six "side effects" or benefits of making a good Confession. Here we consider each of them in turn. Two of them have aspects of reconciliation, which gives us another name for this sacrament.

First, in Confession the penitent is reconciled with God and recovers grace. Whenever we sin mortally we separate ourselves from God. By repenting and confessing our sins and receiving absolution God gives us another chance to begin again and to develop our friendship with Him which all the Saints enjoy.

Second, the penitent is reconciled with the Church. Our sins wound not only ourselves and our relationship with God but also our relationship with Christ's mystical body, the Church.

Third, the penitent is freed from the eternal punishment incurred by mortal sin. Most people who go to Confession (and we should all be going to Confession) have this in mind when entering the confessional. God does not want us to die in our sins and suffer the eternal punishments of Hell. When we well confess our sins we are of one mind with God because of our desire for Heaven.

Fourth, the penitent receives the remission, at least in part, of the temporal punishments due to sin.

While a good Confession can keep us from going to Hell, there is still the "time" in Purgatory to consider, in reparation for venial sins and the like. When we are assigned our various penances these are to alleviate, at least in part, the temporal punishments due to sin. The sacramental absolution also decreases these temporal punishments. Fifth, the penitent receives peace and serenity of conscience together with spiritual consolations. Together with not going to Hell, these benefits of making a good Confession are normally very much present in the minds and hearts of penitents. Who of us does not want peace and serenity of conscience? When we are aware of the foulness and stain of sin on our souls we worry, have trouble sleeping, are irritable... but when we are well confessed, thanks to God's grace powerfully present, all is right at least in our souls.

Sixth, the penitent receives an increase of spiritual strength for the Christian combat, fighting sin and Satan in our hearts and in the world. To keep the devil(s) at bay it is good to have much grace at our disposal.

Frequent reception of the Sacrament of Penance and Holy Communion serves to repulse demonic attacks and keeps us focused on the Lord, in whom we are victorious over sin, Satan, and the glamour of evil. Part of our task as followers of the Lord Jesus involves constant spiritual combat relying upon God's grace at work in us. (cf. CCC, 1496)

13.   In the *Catechism*, as in the *Code of Canon Law* (1983, canons 960-963), Mother Church has us consider five things about the Sacrament of Penance.

First, confession of our grave sins is to be done individually. Individual confession of grave sins is a part of the Sacrament of Penance. The Penitential Rite of Mass, for example, is an ordinary communal means for the forgiveness of venial, lesser sins.

At the Holy Mass we pray "I confess..." and "Lord have mercy" all together.

In the Sacrament of Penance we go individually to the priest confessor to admit our specific and personal need for God's grace and mercy. Grave / Mortal / Serious sins require the Sacrament of Penance as the ordinary means of attaining God's mercy.

Second, confession of our grave sins is to be integral. To make an integral confession of grave sins means to actually say what sins we have committed, 'number and kind.' The reference to 'number and kind' helps to explicate what an integral confession is the "number" refers to how many times the sin was committed, the "kind" refers to the sort of sin committed (e.g. I robbed three banks). If we purposely omit one or another grave sin during confession, that makes the confession sacrilegious, a sin in itself. This is why a thorough examination of conscience should proceed confession. While some people try to justify the omission of one or another sin due to embarrassment, we should rather be embarrassed to die in our sins, spurning God's grace and mercy.

Third, confession of our grave sins is to be followed by the prayer of absolution by the priest. This prayer is an 'effective utterance' and is no less essential than the actual repentant confessing. Our sin(s) affects our personal relationship with God. Through His personal representative on Earth, the priest, the Lord Jesus personally grants us forgiveness.

Fourth, the Sacrament of Penance remains the only ordinary means for reconciliation with God and with His Church. This is how the Lord set up His Church (cf. Matthew 8:4; John 20:23). What sort of hubris (sinful pride!) would be involved for us to tell the Lord how He ought to give us His saving merciful grace?

Finally, by addressing the "ordinary" means for reconciliation with God and His Church in confession, may imply extraordinary means for reconciliation... When soldiers go off to battle, or the plane is crashing, or even as other disasters occur, the Church allows "general absolution" to be given and validly received.

Recourse to the Sacrament of Penance is nonetheless required for subsequent reception of the graces of mercy and forgiveness.

Live in God's grace, faithful to the Sacrament of Penance! (cf. CCC, 1497)

14.   The term "Indulgences" when used by Mother Church refers to the remission of the temporal punishments which are a consequence of our sins. Presupposed are certain specific conditions, such as sacramental confession and absolution, freedom from any attachment to sin and the performance of some particular act. The eternal punishment and guilt due to mortal sin is removed in the Sacrament of Penance, but temporal punishments may remain, exacted in this life or the next (in Purgatory). Some penances assigned might include so many days of fasting or making pilgrimage... temporality is indicated by the inclusion days...

Other understandings of the term "indulgence" which are
opposed to the true Catholic doctrine are highlighted by the *Oxford
Dictionary* such as a luxury which is indulged in or the state or attitude
of being indulgent or tolerant. The Church's doctrine on indulgences
is not "permission to commit as many crimes" as one may wish. That
"Vatican II did away with indulgences" or "Martin Luther did away
with indulgences" does not take into consideration the *Catechism* or
that in 2006 the United States Conference of Catholic Bishops
(USCCB) published the English fourth edition (1999) of the *Manual of
Indulgences, Norms and Grants*, which had been preceded by the 1991
publication in English of the third edition (1986)...

The "poster boy" for the abuses concerning indulgences is said
to be Johann Tetzel (+1519) whose famous rhyme concerning the
simonious "sale of indulgences" runs: *as soon as the gold in the casket
rings, the rescued soul to Heaven springs.*

The sin of simony is the attempt to buy or sell what is holy and is named after Simon Magus who tried to "buy" the power of the Apostles as related in Acts 8:9-24. It is good to recall that Sacred Scripture does include the injunctions that "almsgiving expiates every sin" (Tobit 12:9) and "almsgiving covers a multitude of sins" (Sirach 3:33).

Indulgences may be obtained by the faithful during this life. There are some twenty-six *Norms* governing the current practice of indulgences, together with four general and thirty-three other *Concessions* whereby which the faithful may obtain the desired graces.

The indulgences obtained during this life may be applied to oneself or to the souls in Purgatory. The "Poor Souls" in Purgatory are poor insofar as they are not yet enjoying the bliss of Heaven. Because Purgatory is the anti-chamber of Heaven the souls there are blessed. The souls in purgatory rely upon the communion of saints and the intercession of the Saints in Heaven and the saints still living on Earth.

128

By offering suffrages for the dead we help them on their journey to God and dynamically live out the communion of saints. (cf. CCC, 1498)

15.   The 1983 *Code of Canon Law* and the 1992 *Catechism of the Catholic Church* are attempts to put the Second Vatican Council (1962-1965) into effect, as tools of implementation. Canon 959 highlights for us at least four things about the Sacrament of Penance.

First, we learn that sins committed after Baptism wound both the sinner and the entire Church. While the distinction between mortal / grave / serious and venial sins are not addressed here, all sin is evil even those which are not deadly (cf. 1 John 5:16-17). All sin is an offense against the Holy God who has made us in His image and who calls each of us to holiness (cf. Genesis 1:26; Leviticus 11:44; Matthew 5:48).

Second, penitents are to confess their sins with both sorrow and proposing to reform. The different sorts of sorrow for sin (perfect and imperfect contrition) are not specifically mentioned by the canon. Perfect contrition is sorrow for sin due to the love of God. Imperfect contrition is sorrow for sin due to fear of eternal punishments. It can not be stressed enough, that God does not want any of us to suffer the eternal punishments of Hell and there is nothing imperfect in God (cf. Isaiah 45:22; Ezekiel 3:18; 18:23; Matthew 5:48). God does not force us to repent. God does not force us into His presence. Nothing unclean enters into His eternal presence in Heaven (cf. Revelation 21:27). God wants us to be converted and to live by His grace.

The Sacrament of Penance is the sacrament of the ongoing conversion to which we are all called.

Third, the absolution is imparted by a legitimate minister. The prayer of absolution is the prayer prayed by the priest (or bishop) over the penitent, imparting God's mercy. In order to be a "legitimate minister" of the Sacrament of Penance the priest (or bishop) needs not only to be ordained (at least to the presbyterate / priesthood) but to have "faculties." Priests receive their faculties from their bishop while bishops receive their faculties with episcopal consecration (cf. canon 375 § 2).

Fourth, fruits flowing from the Sacrament of Penance include both obtaining forgiveness from God and reconciliation with the Church. By confessing our sins in the Sacrament of Penance we submit ourselves anew to God and to His gentle yoke and are liberated from servitude to sin (cf. Matthew 11:29-30; John 8:34). Our lives in Christ begin with the saving waters of Baptism through which we are cleansed in the blood of the Lamb (cf. Revelation 7:14).

The graces of innocence and holiness are renewed and we are made clean by the Sacrament of Penance (cf. Matthew 8:3; Mark 1:41-42; Luke 17:11-19). (cf. CIC, 959)

16.   The Sacrament of Penance is a salvific remedy. Jesus Christ uses His sacraments to administer the graces He won by His saving Passion on Good Friday. The specific saving graces administered in the Sacrament of Penance addresses our need for forgiveness of post-baptismal sins.

Certain dispositions are required to receive the sacraments well. Baptism presupposes Faith, at least on the part of the parents and godparents in the case of Infant Baptism. Bread and wine as well as a validly ordained priest are required for Eucharist. When considering the Sacrament of Penance there are three specific dispositions addressed by this canon as being required in order to make a good confession.

132

A prerequisite for the worthy reception of the Sacrament of Penance is that one is a member of the Christian faithful, that is baptized. The Sacrament of Penance is for the remission of post-baptismal sins. Among the graces proper to Baptism, which we have already considered, are not only the forgiveness of Original Sin which we inherit with our human nature, but also the forgiveness of any other sins we may have personally committed before Baptism.

The second required disposition for a worthy reception of the Sacrament of Penance is the repudiation (rejection) of the sins committed. Whenever we sin we choose poorly, we choose evil. Whenever we confess our sins we choose well, we choose God and His grace and mercy. By repudiating and rejecting our sins in the Sacrament of Penance we have the same mind as Christ who also despises sin (cf. Romans 7:25; 15:5-6; 1 Corinthians 1:10; 2:13-16; Philippians 1:27; 1 Peter 1:13).

By renouncing the iniquity, impurity and filth of our sins we cooperate with Christ Jesus who came to destroy the works of the devil and make us adopted children of God, holy and pleasing in His sight (cf. Leviticus 15:31; Deuteronomy 7:26; 13:18; 29:17; Hebrews 13:21; 1 Peter 3:21; 1 John 3:4-10, 22; 4:4; 5:2).

The third required disposition for a worthy reception of the Sacrament of Penance according to the canon is having a purpose of amendment. The Latin version of the *Act of Contrition* actually specifies the sort of amendment of life called for as *firmiter propono* (firmly propose / resolve / intend). Of course, it is with the help of God's grace that we repent our sins and avoid them.

The Sacrament of Penance is a part of the ongoing conversion to which the Lord calls us (cf. Matthew 13:15; 18:3; Luke 17:4). Having been baptized, repudiating our sins and proposing to amend our lives we are converted to the Lord God more and more, day by day, in His saving grace. May it always be so unto eternity. (cf. CIC, 987)

17.   The Christian Faithful are to make a careful examination of conscience (cf. 1 Corinthians 11:28; Galatians 6:4; 1 Peter 3:21). In order to examine our conscience we should look upon the Cross whereupon Jesus died to free us from our sins, the Commandments (Exodus 20:1-17; Deuteronomy 5:4-20), the Beatitudes (cf. Matthew 5:3-12; Luke 6:20-22), the virtues (and the vices; cf. Job 20:11; Psalms 84:7; Proverbs 31:10; Galatians 5:24; Philippians 4:8; 2 Peter 1:5), and the Works of Mercy both corporal and spiritual (cf. Matthew 25:31-46).

The Christian Faithful are bound to confess all grave / mortal / serious sins committed after Baptism according to number and kind ("I did x, y times"). There are three conditions required together for a sin to be grave / mortal / serious: grave matter, committed in full knowledge and deliberately done (cf. CCC, 1957). Grave matter is specified by the Ten Commandments (*Decalogue*; cf. CCC, 1858).

The object, intention, and circumstance should also be considered in a thorough examination of conscience, the object being the objective criteria (cf. CCC, 1750-1754). The best of intentions can not make a bad object good and the worst of circumstances can not make a bad object good.

Individual confession of sins in the Sacrament of Penance allows the power of the keys to be exercised by Mother Church. "The keys of the Kingdom of Heaven" are entrusted to Saint Peter referring to binding and loosening in Heaven and on Earth (cf. Matthew 16:19). Before the Lord Jesus entrusted the keys of the Kingdom to Saint Peter Isaiah had already prophesied about "the key of the House of David" being "upon his shoulder: and he shall open, and no one shall shut: and he shall shut, and none shall open" (22:22), a prophecy cited in the Book of Revelation 3:7. To bind and to loose has been understood as referring to the Sacrament of Penance and the absolution given (or not) in the sacrament.

So long as we come with sorrow in our hearts, not wanting to spend all eternity in Hell, the confessor is bound to grant us absolution, that is, to loosen us from eternal damnation, thanks to the Blood of Jesus shed once for all.

It is also recommended that the Christian Faithful also confess venial sins. That there are deadly or mortal sins, as well as other sins which are not deadly is evident from Sacred Scripture (cf. 1 John 5:16-17). The Sacrament of Penance is necessary for the remission of mortal / deadly sins and is beneficial for the remission of venial sins. If full knowledge is lacking or deliberate choice in freedom is missing from sinful actions or desires then the sins are venial. (cf. CIC, 988)

18. There are five significant consequences of the Sacrament of Penance which we should consider, namely:

In the Sacrament of Penance we receive the mercy of God. Which of us does not want to be right with God?

The signs on the side of the road may make us smile, but we will smile for all eternity in Heaven if we get right with God in the here and now. As Saint Paul wrote, inspired by God: "We implore you on behalf of Christ, be reconciled to God" (2 Corinthians 5:20).

In the Sacrament of Penance we receive from God pardon for offenses committed against Him. Even when we sin against the last seven Commandments of the Decalogue we sin against God who calls us to holiness. We show our love for God and neighbor by keeping His Commandments (cf. John 14:15). Jesus did not come to abolish the Commandments but to give us the grace to keep them, and the grace of mercy for the times when we fail to keep them (cf. Matthew 5:17). We are true friends of the Lord when we keep His Commandments (cf. John 15:14). We are His enemies when we spurn God and His Commandments. The Lord allows us and encourages us to renew our friendship with Him in the Sacrament of Penance.

In the Sacrament of Penance we are reconciled with the Church. Because our sins wound not only ourselves but also Mother Church we also have need to be reconciled with her. This happens in the Sacrament of Penance. We are called to holiness and to be "living stones" in the great edifice which is Mother Church (cf. 1 Peter 2:5). When we are well confessed, when we are in a state of grace, then we are living stones and are being built up in Christ (cf. Ephesians 4:12).

Our sins not only wound ourselves but Christ's Mystical Body, Mother Church. While our sins damage, even possibly unto damnation, ourselves, they also wound the entire Church, of which we are each a part by Baptism. When we fail to live up to the call to holiness received in Baptism we set a bad example for our neighbors as well as head down the wrong path away from God.

Mother Church works for the conversion of sinners on three fronts: charity, example, and prayer.

One of the "Spiritual Works of Mercy" is to "rebuke the sinner" not for rebuke's sake, but to call back from errancy (cf. Psalm 141:5; Matthew 18:15 Saint Augustine, *Enchiridion,* 72; omitted from CCC,2447). The example of how many converted sinners (Saint Augustine comes to mind, among others...) call each of us to repentance and holiness. (cf. CCC, 1422)

19.   Four considerations are worth examining in canon 914:

First, when children are preparing for their first Confession those who are responsible for the task include the parents (including foster or adoptive parents) and the parish priest. If the parents never go to the Sacrament of Penance, there is little chance their children will go. If the parents are faithful to the Sacrament of Penance there is every hope that their children will be faithful similarly. Blessed John Paul II as both priest and bishop (including Bishop of Rome) is said to have approached the Sacrament of Penance each week to confess his sins.

Second, the timing for the first Confession is based, in part, upon the use of reason. Sin is an offense against reason (cf. CCC, 1894). If due to mental incapacity we are not able to discern right from wrong, good from evil, then we also are unable to discern ordinary food from extraordinary food, bread from the Eucharist. In order to well receive Holy Communion we must be able to both discern the Body of the Lord as well as our need for His grace and mercy received in the Sacrament of Penance (cf. 1 Corinthians 11:27-29). The Greek words *dokimazo* and *diakrino* used by Saint Paul, inspired by the Holy Spirit, mean to test, discern, examine, to separate thoroughly, to discriminate, judge. When we receive the Sacrament of Penance we test our consciences against the Ten Commandments, the Beatitudes, the Works of Mercy, the Virtues (and the vices). With the help of the priest confessor we discern and examine our lives before the Cross of Christ and His great mercy and justice.

Third, while a good Confession is part of the proper preparation for first Holy Communion, a good Confession also prepares us for a worthy Holy Communion for those times when we are conscious of any serious / mortal / grave sin(s). In the *Lord's Prayer* we are able to recognize the link between Eucharist and Penance: "give us this day our daily bread... forgive us our trespasses..." (cf. Matthew 6:9-13). We should approach the Sacrament of Penance before receiving Holy Communion for the first time or any subsequent Holy Communions whenever we are conscious of serious / mortal / grave sin(s).

Fourth, the parish priest, through an act of pastoral judgment, must ensure that only those who have reached the use of reason and who are properly disposed receive Holy Communion. While the parents, of course, play a key role in the admission to the sacraments, so too our spiritual Fathers, the priests. The Confessions I have heard in our Catholic Schools for at least eleven years have all been very fruitful. (cf. CIC, 914)

142

20.   Concerning the Sacrament of Penance, there are five things

worthy of consideration in canon 916.

The first consideration concerning canon 916 is the importance

of the examination of conscience whereby we may become conscious

of grave sin. If we never examine our conscience and recognize our

shortcomings and sins, then we will never repent or confess them and

we will die in our sins, thwarting the holy will of God, namely, our

salvation.

A second consideration concerning canon 916 reminds us that

priests and bishops are not to celebrate Mass in grave sin. No one,

laity, priest or bishop... is to receive Holy Communion with grave sin

on the soul. To receive Holy Communion with sin one's soul is called

sacrilegious communion and is itself a grave sin. In order to celebrate

Mass or to receive Holy Communion well, those conscious of grave

sin must first go to the Sacrament of Penance or Confession.

A third consideration concerning canon 916 is that sometimes there may be a grave reason to offer the Holy Mass or to go to Holy Communion and no opportunity to confess before hand. If a priest or bishop has been assigned to such an assignment so as to make impossible for him to make a good Confession, God does not ask the impossible... In my last five assignments as a priest I have not been in such a situation and I have made myself available to penitents wishing to make a good Confession, often hearing an average more than one hundred confessions monthly.

A fourth consideration concerning canon 916 reminds us that the power of a "perfect act of contrition" is not insignificant. The *Act of Contrition* is a part of the Sacrament of Penance but need not be limited to use only in the Sacrament of Penance. Frequent praying of the *Act of Contrition* may keep the both the mercy and justice of God before our eyes and dissuades us from further sins.

The fifth and final consideration of canon 916 is that included in a "perfect act of contrition" is the firm resolve not only to "sin no more" but also to "go to confession as soon as possible." Let us avail ourselves of the Sacrament of Penance often, and with devotion. Blessed John Paul II gave us the excellent example of weekly Confession. To only go to Confession once or twice each year, or God forbid even less frequently, makes a thorough examination of conscience more difficult and sadly increases the risk of dying in a state of mortal sin with dreadful consequences. God's mercy awaits us and our souls are cleansed in the Sacrament of Penance. (cf. CIC, 916)

21.   When considering the Sacrament of Penance we should recall the three "Acts of the Penitent" namely: contrition, confession and satisfaction. Here we focus on contrition.

The Hebrew word *shabar* and the Latin word *contritio* mean a breaking of something hardened.

To be contrite is to be broken hearted over our sins, remembering that Jesus Christ had His Sacred Heart Pierced for love of us and our redemption (cf. Psalm 34:18; 51:17; Isaiah 57:15; 61:1; Jeremiah 5:23; Ezekiel 3:7). The Lord Jesus Christ rebuked the eleven after the resurrection because of their hardness of heart (cf. Mark 16:14) even as He corrected the Pharisees who rejected the indissoluble nature of Marriage (cf. Matthew 19:1-12)

A contrite person experiences a sorrow of soul. The sorrow is for the offense given to Almighty God who is all good and deserving of all our love and obedience. That God is deserving of all our love and obedience is to recall His sovereignty over His creation of which we are a part. This is not just for external show but deeply interior and not just psychological but based on supernatural motivations. We are not to just be sorry for one or another sin but for all of our sins.

A contrite person detests the sins committed. The Hebrew word *sane* is sometimes translates hate while *taab* is to loathe or abhor. To detest, hate, loathe or abhor something is pretty serious.

Sacred Scripture when addressing idiolatry exhorts us to detest idols as dung (cf. Deuteronomy 7:26). Elsewhere we read that God detests arrogance, pride, evil and every wicked way (cf. Proverbs 8:13; Amos 5:15; 6:8). As His people so should we. We are directed to both love the Lord and to hate evil (cf. Psalm 97:10). Saint Paul, inspired by the Holy Spirit admits that he did not do the good he willed but the evil that he hated (cf. Romans 7:15).

A contrite person resolves with the help of God's grace to sin no more in the future. When we have a true sorrow for our sins it is in part because we have recognized our sins and God's great mercy and justice. We know that grace and truth come to us from Christ who is the way, the truth and the life, who gives us access to the hope of glory with God in Heaven as adopted and redeemed sons and daughters (cf. John 1:17; 14:6; Romans 5:2).

Let us all pray, asking for God's grace to be truly sorry for all our sins so as to receive God's forgiveness in the Sacrament of Penance.

Then we will be pleasing in His sight here and now and in the

hereafter! (cf. CCC, 1451)

22.	There are two aspects highlighting the human and

psychological value of confession, namely freedom and reconciliation.

The Sacrament of Penance is not a counseling session. Spiritual

Direction may have aspects of counseling, but is altogether different

from both psychology (which examines perceptions, motivations,

behaviors and the like) and psychiatry (which is a medical field to

diagnose, treat, and prevent mental disorders). The manifestation of

conscience, freely made in the confessional or to a counselor, often has

a freeing consequence. When guilt is acknowledged in confession to

another the possibility of reconciliation is a reality. Doctors of

Psychology or Psychiatry, unless they are priests with the faculty to

absolve, are unable to grant the pardon which can only come from God

who is offended by each of our sins and all of our sins.

Care for the eternal disposition of the soul before God is specific to the Sacrament of Penance.

There are four aspects highlighting the dynamics of the Sacrament of Penance, namely looking squarely at the sins which we commit, assumption of our responsibility as doers of evil, openness to God and His mercy, and openness to the possibility of a new future.

The first dynamic of making a good Confession requires us to look squarely at the sins which we have committed. There is no sugar-coating here. We call a spade a spade and sin a sin. God's holy Law helps us to recognize sin for what it is (cf. Romans 7:7). This is difficult in a day and age when there seems to be the 'loss of the sense of sin' when people say 'there is no such thing as sin' which robs the Cross of it's power to save (cf. 1 Corinthians 1:17-18; Galatians 5:11).

The second dynamic of making a good Confession is to assume responsibility for the evil we have done. We have done what we have done (or not done what we should have done...). Some people might call this 'reality therapy.'

To acknowledge our sins is an essential part of the Sacrament of Penance (cf. Psalm 32:5; 51:3; Jeremiah 3:13; 14:20; Proverbs 14:9; 2 Samuel 19:20).

The third dynamic of making a good Confession is to be open to God and His mercy. We believe that God is both just and merciful, Who wants us to be saved, to call upon Him in trusting faith (cf. Acts 2:21; Romans 10:12-13). We do this in the Sacrament of Penance.

The final dynamic of making a good Confession regards the new future which is opened up by a good Confession. This includes not only peace of conscience in the here and now but also life on high with Christ Jesus and all His saints. (cf. CCC, 1455)

23. We can never stress enough the importance of a thorough examination of conscience. How should we go about examining our conscience? Five different tools are at our ready disposal with which we can be sure to thoroughly examine our consciences and make a good, integral Confession, namely:

We examine our conscience before the Cross of the Lord. This is because Jesus Christ died on the Cross, on Calvary, on Good Friday because of my sins, and your sins, and the sins of every person who ever has been and ever will be. To examine our conscience is to recognize the part we played and our responsibility for His sorrowful Passion.

We examine our conscience before the Commandments of God. The *Catechism* specifically mentions "the last two precepts of the Decalogue" (not to covet the neighbors wife, not to covet the neighbors goods) as being important matter for confession. There are several reasons for especially confessing sins against the last two commandments. For example when we sin in other ways others may well rebuke us "hey, don't say that... don't steal / take that... don't hit that person"... The last two Commandments treat sins in the heart and mind. If left there, unattended by God's healing grace made available to us in the Sacrament of Penance they will fester and rot, causing destruction from within.

We examine our conscience before the Beatitudes. In the *Sermon on the Mount* the Commandments of God are taken to the next level by Jesus Christ the Lord (cf. Matthew 5:1-7:29). The Beatitudes are at the heart of the *Sermon on the Mount* (cf. Matthew 5:3-11). Our roadmap to holiness includes being poor in spirit (humble), mournful (for our own sins and those of our neighbors, with others who mourn...)

We examine our conscience before the Works of Mercy, both Corporal and Spiritual. Sins which should be confessed are not just evil deeds done or desired, but also the good things we failed to do. Feeding the hungry, clothing the naked, rebuking the sinner, instructing the ignorant... these are the things we are called to do as manifestations of our friendship with the Lord Jesus.

We examine our conscience before the virtues and vices. The virtues correspond to our very human nature, the root being the Latin word for man, *vir*. The natural virtues, both Cardinal virtues and moral virtues correspond to our human nature.

God made us to be prudent, and just, and temperate and strong (fortitude). The supernatural graces given in Baptism are the origins of the supernatural, theological virtues of Faith, Hope, and Charity. These are attacked and wounded by our sins but God mercifully restores them in the Sacrament of Penance. (cf. CCC, 1456)

24.   There are three "acts of the penitent" which should be examined when considering the Sacrament of Penance: contrition, confession and satisfaction. Having already focused on contrition and confession, we now look at satisfaction.

Among the many various important considerations we should make, one concerns "satisfaction." Satisfaction is made through reparation and is a part of the Sacrament of Penance.

Merriam-Webster reminds us that satisfaction addresses "the temporal punishment incurred by a sin" meeting "the demands of divine justice" and that reparation is "the act of making amends, offering expiation, or giving satisfaction for a wrong or injury" including "the payment of damages." When it comes to our salvation and redemption it is Christ Jesus who paid the ultimate price on His Cross. We only contribute what we can, thanks to His grace at work in us, as we repent and make amends as we are able.

One form of satisfaction is made through restitution of stolen things and is a part of the Sacrament of Penance. In restoring stolen good the owner receives what is due. God is due our love, respect and obedience. Another form of satisfaction is made through rehabilitation of the reputation of one who was slandered this too is a part of the Sacrament of Penance. In this way we attempt to right the wrong we have done by speech. Still another form of satisfaction is also made through compensation for wounds inflicted and make up a part of the Sacrament of Penance.

These are all simply parts of natural justice, giving each their due. God too has His due. Our sins, however, not only often wound others, they always wound us, as well as our relations with both God and neighbor. The Sacrament of Penance gives forgiveness and restores spiritual holiness, imparted especially in the absolution. There are consequences of our sins which are addressed by our penances, the satisfaction we offer. The penances and satisfactions we "offer up" figure in to the "temporal punishment" due to sin. Either we make timely amends in this life or in Purgatory, or forever in Hell.

The Sacrament of Penance is a remedy and means of salvation for the repentant.

When we are assigned one or another prayer or practice(s) by the priest confessor in the Sacrament of Penance, we are making 'satisfaction' for our sins, uniting our labors to Christ's victorious labor of Good Friday. Of course, there is nothing we can do to earn, buy or deserve God's grace and mercy.

When we do which ever works of penance, of satisfaction, we show God both the depths of our sorrow as well as our willingness to make things right, thanks to His grace(s). (cf. CCC, 1459)

25.   Holy Mother Church recognizes the differences between sins as found in Sacred Scripture: "He that knows his brother to sin a sin which is not to death, let him ask: and life shall be given to him who sins not to death. There is a sin unto death. For that I say not that any man ask. All iniquity is sin. And there is a sin unto death" (1 John 5:16-17). Another way of speaking about death involves terms like mortal and mortality. This is where we get the expression "mortal sin." The "Seven Deadly Sins" or "Capital Sins" correspond to the vices of pride, avarice (or greed), envy, wrath (or anger), lust, gluttony, and sloth (cf. CCC 1866). The entire third section of the *Catechism of the Catholic Church* addresses moral issues in even greater detail.

Saint Thomas Aquinas, O.P. (+1274), priest and Doctor of the Church, is always a safe and expert source to help us further understand the mysteries of faith and redemption. There are over one hundred references to "mortal" and "venial" sin in his master work *Summa Theologiae*. In part, Saint Thomas Aquinas teaches that without penance it is impossible for an actual mortal sin to be pardoned, if we speak of penance as a virtue. Sin is an offense against God who pardons sin in the same way as He pardons an offense committed against Him" that is, personally (cf. ST III, Q. 86, A. 1). Every mortal sin is opposed to grace and excludes grace and requires both true penance and the renunciation of sin. All mortal sins are against God (cf. ST III, Q. 86, A. 3). Our mortal sins exclude us from the good of glory for which God made us and for which Christ suffered and died to redeem us (cf. ST III, Q. 86, A. 3 ad 5). Mortal sin gives rise to the debt of eternal punishment as an appropriate response to our rejection of the greatest, most perfect Good who is God (cf. ST III, Q. 86, A. 4).

Venial sins involve a disorder or defect in our desires and deeds but not to the same degree as mortal sins (cf. ST I-II, Q. 88, A. 1). The disorder and defect introduced by mortal sins are such that the grace of God is required for the repair to be made. Venial sins merit temporal punishment whereas mortal sins merit everlasting punishment (cf. ST I-II, Q. 88, A. 2).

The *Good News* of our salvation and redemption in Christ is the possibility of pardon of both mortal and venial sins, thanks to God's grace readily available in the Sacrament of Penance (cf. ST III, Q. 86, A. 4 ad 1). (cf. CCC, 1845)

26.   Six considerations help us to appreciate the need we have for the Sacrament of Penance, three addressing mortal sin, two addressing venial sin, and one regarding our ultimate end.

First we should recall that mortal sin destroys charity in the human heart. If we recall that "God is love" (*Deus Caritas Est*) this is a very stark teaching (cf. 1 John 4:16).

158

The life of God in us is snuffed out by our mortal sin(s). In the Sacrament of Penance, when we confess our sins with sorrow in our hearts and receive absolution, God in His great mercy, restores in our hearts the grace of charity.

Second we should recall that mortal sin is committed by a grave infraction of the Law of God. When we confess our sins in the Sacrament of Penance we follow God's law of mercy, submitting ourselves anew to His gentle yoke.

Third, we should recall that mortal sin turns us away from God. It is not enough to recognize the destruction of charity in our hearts caused by mortal sin. By choosing to sin grievously we choose poorly against following Jesus Christ who is "the way, the truth and the life" (cf. John 14:6).

Fourth, we should always recall that God is our ultimate end and our beatitude. Because of God's omniscience (all knowing attribute) He foresees our need for post-baptismal repentance.

The Sacrament of Penance is here in order for us to get to Heaven, to spend all eternity with God who has made us for Himself. Whenever we sin we prefer something which is not God to God, which is disordered. When we make a good confession we recognize God's good order and reject sin and Satan and the glamour of evil. Apart from God and His plan for us any happiness is only apparent and passing.

Fifth, we should recall that while venial sin does allow charity to subsist in the human heart it nevertheless offends God and His holiness. This is to say we should avoid even venial sin as best we can, thanks to God's grace at work in us.

Finally, we should recall that venial sin as an offense against God wounds our relationship with Him. One problem with venial sin is that it desensitizes us to sin. The Chinese method of torture and execution *ling chih* or "death by a thousand cuts" comes to mind here. Countless venial sins never add up to a single mortal sin but the coarseness of our hearts increase through repeated venial sin.

160

The Lord Jesus has given us a remedy in the Sacrament of Penance to combat post-baptismal sin in our lives so as to be pleasing in His sight. (cf. CCC, 1855)

27.   How do we know what is a mortal sin? Holy Mother Church teaches us that there are three criteria which must be present together in order for a sin to be a mortal sin, namely: grave matter, full knowledge, deliberately done. We will consider each of these.

In order for a sin to be a "mortal sin" that which is done or omitted must be "grave matter." Grave Matter is made precise by the Ten Commandments or Decalogue. While all theft is sinful, it should be obvious that to steal a pin used for sewing is not as serious a crime as stealing an automobile. While it is bad to abuse the pets it is worse to abuse the children or the defenseless. Another way to say "grave" is "serious." There is nothing frivolous about mortal sin.

In order for a sin to be a "mortal sin" we must have "full knowledge" knowing what we are doing.

Normally, if we have reached the age of reason (about seven years old) and are not mentally impaired we are responsible for the good we do (or fail to do) or the evil we commit.

In order for a sin to be a "mortal sin" the deed or omission must be done deliberately. This is not to say that if you burn someone's home down, (itself grave matter of which we should be aware as a subset of Seventh Commandment: Thou shall not steal, insofar as one's property rights are infringed upon), but the people were inside unknown to you, the deaths of the people, further grave matter (Fifth Commandment: Thou shall not kill), while obviously serious were not intended. Sometimes coercion has been mentioned as affecting the quality of our deliberateness. Imagine an employer threatening to fire the employee if reports are not falsified. The employee who is normally an honest person might be coerced to lie in order to remain employed. While it would be heroic to resist such an employer, the personal culpability would be lessened in such a circumstance.

Regardless, the falsification of the reports remain a grave matter
(Eighth Commandment: Thou shall not bear false witness).

One sad consequences of Original Sin is the difficulty we have
knowing the truth about ourselves, about God, about good and evil.
Thankfully God has revealed the Decalogue or Ten Commandments to
us as an expression of the Natural Law which we are able to know
thanks to the light of natural human reason. (cf. CCC, 1858, 1957)

The lifting up of the seraph serpent on a pole by Moses at God's command is a prefiguration of Christ's being lifted up on the wood of the Cross (cf. John 3:14). The caduceus has been a symbol of medical care (cf. Numbers 21:5-9). While the grace of the sacraments are primarily for spiritual healing, sometimes the Lord gives miracles.

ANOINTING

1.   "Is there any one among you who is sick? Then call the
      presbyters of the Church and they will pray over him, after
      having anointed him with oil in the Name of the Lord. The
      prayer of faith will save the patient, and the Lord will raise
      Him. If he has committed any sins, they will be remitted"
      (Saint James 5:14-15).

This passage from the New Testament is included as a part of

the Rite of the Sacrament of Penance. At the Council of Trent (AD

1551) Mother Church recognized explicitly this passage as an

admonition to the Sacrament of the Anointing of the Sick administered

by priests to those who are in danger of death due to advanced age or

illness. The sacrament is administered fruitfully also to those not yet

at death's door. Sacred Scripture reminds us that the medicinal

properties of oil were recognized in antiquity (cf. Isaiah 1:6; Mark

6:13; Luke 10:34). The Greek words *aleipho* and *chrio* refer to the

general practice in ancient times of rubbing the body with oil or grease

seeking relief from sun burn.

The healing which goes on in the Sacrament of the Anointing of the Sick is always spiritual and sometimes physical. Physicality is always involved through the imposition of hands and the anointing with the Oil of the Sick. Jesus Christ is the Divine Physician who heals us of our spiritual ills. He did work miracles during His life on this Earth and works them still through the intercession of His Saints and His bride Mother Church. The Holy Name of Jesus is invoked by Mother Church in the Sacrament of the Anointing of the Sick because He is the prime agent in all of His sacraments, which apply the graces He won on Calvary's Cross.

The use by Saint James of the term "presbyters", which means "elder" or "elderly man" (from the Greek *presbyteros*) is key in identifying the minister of the Sacrament of the Anointing of the Sick. The English word "priest" is derived from the Greek term *presbyteros*.

The priest imposes hands and anoints but the Sacrament of the Anointing of the Sick imparts the grace of God (the Holy Spirit especially) who is the prime actor in all of the sacraments (cf. Luke 4:18; Acts 4:27; 10:38; 2 Corinthians 1:21; Hebrews 19). While the Sacrament of Holy Orders is treated elsewhere by the *Catechism* this passage is not insignificant nor unrelated to other key passages (cf. Acts 14:23; 15:2; 20:17; 21:18).

That the sick person will be saved through the imposition of hands and the anointing by the priest as asserted here reminds us of the role of the sacraments in our eternal salvation. (cf. CCC, 1526)

2.   Sacraments are signs, instituted by Christ, entrusted to the Church to give grace. The Sacrament of the Anointing of the Sick is one of the two Sacraments of Healing, the other being Penance (also called Confession and Reconciliation).

168

The goal or reason for celebrating the Sacrament of the Anointing of the Sick is confer special graces needed by someone who is gravely ill or of advanced age.

What are the special graces conferred by the Sacrament of the Anointing of the Sick? Sometimes the Lord Jesus, the Divine Physician, actually cures or heals the sick person restoring perfect health. Jesus' miracles are His prerogative. He can work them when He will, where He will, as He wills. While we have no right to any miracle, sometimes they happen... Another grace proper to the Sacrament of the Anointing of the Sick is the uniting of our sufferings to those of Christ on His Cross.

Saint Paul, inspired by the Holy Spirit puts it this way: we should rejoice in our sufferings, filling up that which is wanting in the sufferings of Christ (cf. Colossians 1:24). This is not to imply that Good Friday was not enough. But the sufferings we undergo are no less real or significant.

The Lord Jesus, through the Sacrament of the Anointing of the Sick unites our sufferings in the here and now, to His redemptive sufferings, allowing us to participate in the redemption.

Elsewhere in Sacred Scripture we read that to the extent that we partake of the sufferings of Christ we can rejoice that when His glory shall be revealed, we may be glad with exceeding joy (cf. 1 Peter 4:13). The Sacrament of the Anointing of the Sick unites our sufferings to those of Christ, giving us a measure of joy in the here and now as well as a well founded hope for future, eternal, joys.

Two indications as to the timing of the Sacrament of the Anointing of the Sick are given, namely grave illness and old or advanced age. We need not wait until the last moments before death to receive this sacrament. Upon becoming gravely or seriously ill, visit or call the priest and receive the graces you need to endure the trials at hand (cf. James 5:14-15). I can not understand why anyone would not want to have the special graces available in the sacrament for themselves or their loved ones.

Advanced or old age, all things being equal, is a proximate cause of death. In this sense the Sacrament of the Anointing of the Sick is administered for both healing of body and soul, preparing for the final journey to Heaven. Mercy is given to the unconscious who receive this sacrament. (cf. CCC, 1527)

3.   The *Catechism* mentions twice "sickness" and "old age" in connection with the Sacrament of the Anointing of the Sick. In particular, these two situations, sickness and old age are highlighted in connection with the opportune time to receive the Sacrament of the Anointing of the Sick as proximate causes of death.

Christ the Lord instituted His sacraments to give us the grace we need to be the saints He calls us to be. While the Sacrament of the Anointing of the Sick is not only for the dying, it is a source of consolation for those who are dying. What greater comfort could a follower of the Lord Jesus Christ have than to be "fortified" or strengthened by the sacraments.

Not all sicknesses end in death. Just because someone is old enough to join the AARP (American Association of Retired Persons) does not necessarily mean that death is immanent. Sometimes, however, death does result from serious illness. The older we get the closer we are to death. The Sacrament of the Anointing of the Sick gives us the graces we need to face death in the here and now. We know by faith that death is not the end of our lives. Good Friday is not the end of the Gospel. We believe in the resurrection of Christ and we look forward to our own resurrection on the last day. We know the soul continues on after death and proceeds to the judgment seat of Christ. How pleased He will be to see our souls gleaming with the fresh glow of His grace given in the Sacrament of the Anointing of the Sick. We need not be afraid of death, especially when we are in a state of grace. We should always be ready for death. The Sacrament of the Anointing of the Sick when it does not cure us, at least gives us the grace to be ready for death.

There are further rites which while not a part of the sacrament often accompany the Anointing, namely the Apostolic Pardon and the Commendation of the Dying. The priest is only able to pray these prayers when the sick or elderly person is *in extremis* (at the extremity of life, that is dying). A plenary indulgence is attached to the Apostolic Pardon which reminds me of the "get out of jail free" card made famous by the *Monopoly* board game. Jesus Christ has actually paid the price of our redemption and His grace is applied to us in our moment of need in the sacraments. The "Commendation of the Dying" gives the dying person "permission" to go see God who has made us and redeemed us and dwells in us by His grace. (cf. CCC, 1528)

4.   "Each time that a Christian falls greatly sick, he can receive the Holy Anointing, even when, after having received it, if the sickness becomes more grave."

The *Catechism* is at pains here to remind us that just because someone has already received the Sacrament of the Anointing of the Sick before, this does not preclude further reception(s) of the same sacrament. Imagine someone saying, I have already received Holy Communion so I won't receive it any more or again... This is not to say that we should necessarily receive the holy anointing every day. While the *Lord's Prayer* does teach us about receiving "our daily bread" there is no such doctrine concerning a daily anointing. It is not a disparaging of the Eucharist or Anointing that these sacraments are repeated, unlike Baptism, Confirmation and Orders which leave a permanent mark on the soul of the recipient as Saint Thomas Aquinas, OP (+1274) points out (cf. ST Sup. Q. 33, A. 1).

There are two things to consider here: If you or a loved one is greatly sick or ill seek out the Anointing of the Sick. Aquinas further reminds us that this sacrament should not be given to every sick person without any consideration of the degree or stage of illness (cf. ST Sup. Q. 32, A.2).

If you or your loved one have been anointed and the sickness or illness becomes worse, you may be anointed again for the strengthening of your body and soul. While physical healing may not always result from the Sacrament of the Anointing of the Sick, all of the sacraments confer grace, and grace effects the forgiveness of sins for spiritual healing (cf. ST Sup. Q. 30, A. 1-2). The Apostles even before the redemption worked miracles of healing through God's power and anointing (cf. Mark 6:13). Nevertheless, bodily health is not the principal effect of the Anointing of the Sick. Now after the redemption the Divine power and grace of the sacrament is not less effective. While the Sacrament of Penance is the specific sacrament for the remission of the post-baptismal sins we sadly commit, especially for those who have become unconscious, the grace conferred by the holy anointing is not negligible.

I know of one person in our Parish who has been anointed by me at least seven times, during trips to the hospital, during communal celebrations of the sacrament, before surgery and the like.

After my priestly ordination I anointed my grandmother Gertrude Genevieve MacVeany (Vovo) every time I saw her. Her advanced age, she was already 90 years old, was a proximate cause of death and reason enough for anointing. By God's grace she lived 102.80 years on the good Earth. (cf. CCC, 1529)

5.   The *Catechism* addresses both the matter and the minister of the Sacrament of the Anointing of the Sick, namely, the Oil of the Sick and the priest. Latter, the *Catechism* addresses the form of the sacrament.

The minister of the Sacrament of the Anointing of the Sick is either a bishop or a priest. Baptism can validly be administered by anyone in cases of emergency. While the canonical form of Marriage requires the presence of a cleric (bishop, priest or deacon), the bride and groom are actually the ministers of the sacrament.

The necessity of a priest for the Sacrament of the Anointing of the Sick is explicitly mentioned in Sacred Scripture, where we read:

> "Is there anyone sick among you? Send for the priests of the Church and let them pray over the sick person, anointing him with oil in the Name of the Lord..." (James 5:14)

The Greek word *presbuteros* translates as "elder" and is the origin of the word "priest."

The matter of the Sacrament of the Anointing of the Sick is blessed oil. The Oil of the Sick is ideally blessed by the bishop during the Mass of the Chrism during Holy Week (together with the Oil of Catechumens and Sacred Chrism). In cases of emergency even the priest himself may bless the Oil of the Sick. The oil used is ideally olive oil. An innovation or accommodation promulgated by Paul VI in his *Apostolic Constitution Sacram Unctione Infirmorum* (30 November, 1972) allows any plant oil to be used once blessed.

The preference for olive oil is based upon Sacred Scripture (cf. Exodus 27:20; Leviticus 24:2; Deuteronomy 8:8; 28:40; 2 Kings 18:32; 1 Chronicles 27:28). The olive tree is called "king" of the trees (cf. Judges 9:8-9). The plentiful harvest of olive oil has been seen as a great blessing (cf. Joel 2:24; 3:13). The patient labor required for the maturation of an olive tree has been likened to God's patience with His people and the abundant rich fruit as a reward. The olive tree has served as an emblem of peace not only after the flood but also because of the generations required for cultivation (cf. Genesis 8:11). The delicate nature of peace is strikingly represented by the olive tree in that what takes years to mature an army can destroy in a day. Jesus Christ is the Prince of Peace, who has made peace between Heaven and Earth, between us and God by His death and resurrection. That olive oil is produced by the crushing the olive in a mill might remind us of Christ who suffered so on Good Friday. The sick are united to Christ's sufferings in the Sacrament of the Anointing of the Sick. (cf. CCC, 1530)

178

6.   When considering the sacraments, it is good to know their

"matter and form." The matter of the Sacrament of the Anointing of

the Sick is the Oil of the Sick. The form of the sacrament is another

thing. The actual form of the Sacrament of the Anointing of the Sick

is: "Through this holy anointing may the Lord in His love and mercy

help you with the grace of the Holy Spirit" (while anointing the

forehead) and "May the Lord who frees you from sin save you and

raise you up" (while anointing the hands).

A further innovation promulgated by Paul VI in his *Apostolic

Constitution Sacram Unctione Infirmorum* (30 November, 1972)

limited the number a of anointings to three in the Latin Rite.

The sick person is anointed on the forehead and on the palm of each

hand. When priests receive the Anointing of the Sick, the back of the

hand (not the palms) is anointed, their palms already having been

anointed and consecrated with Sacred Chrism in Ordination. The

Eastern Rites have maintained additional anointing (e.g. feet, ears,

eyes, ears...).

The idea being the application of redemptive and healing graces as needed wherever sin may have been committed.

There are likewise further prayers and gestures which are also used in this sacrament. One gesture is the silent imposition of hands upon the head of the sick person preceding the anointing, which allows the Divine Physician to do His work from the inside out. There are still further prayers which accompany the rite. These include the Lord's Prayer and a concluding prayer. The concluding prayer in the Sacrament of the Anointing of the Sick varies according to the circumstances (general illness, before surgery, in advanced age, grave illness...). These prayers all ask of God special graces, physically and spiritually according to God's good pleasure, to be given in the sacrament.

The Sacrament of the Anointing of the Sick unites the sufferings of our lives to the sufferings of Christ and allow us a further participation in the redemption of the world, ourselves included.

180

Saint Paul wrote, inspired by the Holy Spirit, about filling up what was lacking in the sufferings of Christ in our own flesh (cf. Colossians 1:24). This is not to say that Good Friday was not enough to save us all. But, as the Lord filled the net of Apostles after His resurrection He also asked them to "bring some of the fish you have just caught." So the Lord seeks our participation and cooperation even through illness, suffering and death (cf. John 21:10). He cares for us and longs to raise us up, not only from our sins and sufferings in this life but even to eternity. (cf. CCC, 1531)

7.   Each of the sacraments impart specific graces. Five special graces or "side effects" of the Sacrament of the Anointing of the Sick are highlighted in the *Catechism* for our consideration.

A first grace imparted by the Sacrament of the Anointing of the Sick unites the sick person to the Passion of Christ, for personal benefit and the good of the whole Church.

While our aches and pains are ours we are able to endure them by God's grace not only for our own good but for that of the entire Mystical Body of Christ which is the Church. It is far better for us to suffer in the here and now than for all eternity. The Anointing allows us to be united with Christ and His Church.

A second grace imparted by the Sacrament of the Anointing of the Sick gives comfort, peace and the courage to bear like a Christian the sufferings of sickness or old age. To receive comfort from the Anointing presupposes the first grace, namely union with Christ and His Church. What greater comfort might we receive than to be one with Christ? The peace received from the Anointing may well stem from 'being right with God.' What have we to fear if we are one with Christ, crucified and glorified? The courage imparted by the Anointing allows us to face the difficulties of sickness and old age as true followers of Christ. The holy martyrs have all lived these graces of comfort, peace and courage.

A third grace imparted by the Sacrament of the Anointing of the Sick gives the pardon or forgiveness of sins not already obtained in the Sacrament of Penance. The 'Continuous Rite' of this sacrament actually includes the confession of sins and absolution. If, however, the sick person is unconscious and thereby unable to confess, the merciful graces of God are made available. If we are able to confess our sins we should confess them so that the graces of this sacrament may be rather directed to the alleviation of any temporal punishments due to our sins.

A fourth grace imparted by the Sacrament of the Anointing of the Sick occurs when for the spiritual well-being and salvation of the sick person, health may be reestablished. While not everyone who is anointed receives a physiological cure, sometimes, for the good of our redemption the Good God allows a cure that reparations may be made before breathing one's last.

Finally, the Sacrament of the Anointing of the Sick prepares the sick person to pass from this life to life everlasting in Heaven.

Confidence should be high for those who die, fortified with the grace

of the sacraments. Pray for the grace of a happy death. (cf. CCC,

1532)

184

The Lord Jesus worked His first sign or miracle at the Wedding feast

at Cana changing 180 gallons of water into wine (John 2:1-11). This

anticipates the Eucharist where He changes bread and wine into

Himself as well as the eschatological wedding feast of the Lamb (cf.

Revelation 19:9). Married love between husband and wife is the

primordial sacrament (TOB, 97; 6 October, 1982) which the Lord

elevated among the baptized to the dignity of a sacrament.

MARRIAGE

1.   "Saint Paul says: Husbands, love your wives, as Christ has loved the Church. (...) This mystery is of great range; I say to you that it is applied to Christ and to His Church (Ephesians 5:25, 32)."

This is how the *Catechism* begins its' summary of the dogma concerning Holy Marriage. Beginning these reflections on Holy Marriage, starting with Sacred Scripture, reminds us that the most frequently cited source in the *Catechism* is Sacred Scripture. While Saint Paul's inspired directive does not positively say that "wives should love their husbands" it should be understood. The omitted text, represented by the ellipsis, refers to wives being submissive to their husbands, often celebrated by the chauvinistic. Mutual subjection, anticipating each other in showing respect (cf. Romans 12:10) is what is called for.

How is it that Christ loved His Church? He gave Himself up to death on the Cross. Jesus Christ was not only willing to die for her, He did so. This is a tall order, but part of the sacrificial nature of Holy Marriage as Mother Church sees it. How often mothers of families have died in bringing new life to birth? Saint Gianna Beretta Molla (AD 1922-1962) comes to mind.

Saint Jerome's *Vulgate* renders our English "great mystery" as "*magnum sacramentum.*" Marriage is a great sacrament which makes great saints out of those who are faithful to the call.

The nuptial bond between Christ and His bride is unbreakable. There are some in this world who look at Marriage as if it were only a human construct, able to be toyed with according to the whim and fashion of the day, that is foreign to God's vision and plan.

The word "love" is found in Sacred Scripture in over two hundred verses, one hundred of these in the New Testament. The word "charity" is found another eighty-seven times, eighty-three of these in the New Testament.

Two further magnificent passages help to clarify what God means for us to understand when inspiring Saint Paul to write to the Ephesians "husbands love your wives": 1 John 4:8 and 1 Corinthians 13:1-13.

"He that loves not knows not God: for God is charity" (1 John 4:8) helps us to understand what it means when we read about husbands loving their wives. We have been made in the image of God who is love (charity) and are called to love not only God but neighbor and self. Spouses, by the grace of Holy Marriage are called to especially to love each other.

Saint Paul's "Ode to Charity" (1 Corinthians 13:1-13) helps us to understand what it means when we read about husbands loving their wives. Kindness, humility, generosity, chastity..., these are all manifestations of the love proper to Holy Marriage. (cf. CCC, 1659)

2.   In referring to Holy Marriage as a "matrimonial alliance" or "covenant" the *Catechism* is calling our attention to the sacredness and significance of Holy Marriage. Recall the various covenants throughout sacred history: Noah (cf. Genesis 8:15-9:17), Abraham (cf. Genesis 17:5-14), Moses (cf. Exodus 34:27-28). The bride, the groom, and God enter into a sacred contract, Holy Marriage, upon which they stake their lives.

Christ the Lord, bridegroom of Mother Church, has already laid down His life for us. He was faithful even to His last breath and last drop of blood. He calls husbands and wives to the same faithfulness.

There was a time when the Church's teaching regarding Holy Marriage being a sacred contract (or covenant or alliance) between one man and one woman was not entirely counter cultural, in our days, defense of this aspect of Holy Marriage allows the faithful to share in the prophetic task. The Church's teaching identifying Holy Marriage as existing only between one man and one woman was a challenge to polygamy, which allowed for multiple wives.

When considering the intimacy and the communion of life and love proper to Holy Marriage at least three (3) things should be remembered: intimacy is not limited to lacey undergarments or the nuptial embrace but also includes the sharing of hopes and dreams, joys and sorrows...; communion of life includes but is not limited to actually living together in harmony; communion of love includes but is not limited to willing the good for the other.

It was "in the beginning" that Holy Marriage was founded by the Creator, in creating us male and female and directing fruitfulness and multiplication (cf. Genesis 1:28). The use of the term "Creator" here is intentional, because this teaching is true for all of humanity, not just pious Jews or Christians.

Holy Marriage has been endowed by the Creator with certain properties which include mutual help and support, not only of the spouses for each other, but also for their children.

The proper laws of the Creator regarding Holy Marriage include but are not limited to unity (forsaking all others), indissolubility (life long), fecundity (openness to fertility which implies heterosexuality),

There are two goals or ends of Holy Marriage: The good of the spouses and the generation and education of children.

The good of the spouses includes not only temporal goods such as a roof over the head and clothes on the back and food in our stomachs but also the eternal good which is Heaven. Husband and wife are to help each other, with God's grace, get to Heaven.

The Lord Jesus Christ elevated Holy Marriage among the Baptized to the dignity of a sacrament. The presence of Jesus at Canna, shows His special love for Marriage (cf. John 2:1-11). (cf. CCC. 1660)

3.　　Some people sadly see Marriage as only a human construct, discounting both the divine origins of the human race and of Holy Marriage. People of faith, followers of Jesus Christ recognize that the Sacrament of Marriage has its' signification from God. The union of husband and wife is a relationship unlike any other.

Sacramentally, the primary signification of Holy Marriage is the union of Christ and His Church. Christ is the bridegroom of His bride Mother Church. In Holy Baptism we are born anew from the font which is akin to the womb of the Church. Building upon the graces received in Baptism, Christian husbands and wives receive further graces flowing from their valid exchange of the vows of Holy Marriage, such that, they mirror the bond which exists between the Lord and His mystical body.

The *Catechism* highlights four specific graces proper to the Sacrament of Marriage which we should consider.

The first grace proper to Holy Marriage allows the spouses to love with the love with which Christ has loved His Church. Christ's love for His Church is a faithful love, a fruitful love, a love unto death. Thanks to the grace given to the husband and wife when they validly profess the holy vows of Holy Marriage their love is consecrated and divinized, that is, made holy.

A second grace proper to Holy Marriage perfects the human love of the spouses. What is proper to the human love of spouses? What draws this man and this woman together to form a life long bond? Human love begins for some people with an appreciation of the sense of humor, or the intelligence, or appearance, shared experiences... Like the chef Emeril Lagasse, who is famous for putting in spices, BAM!, so the grace of God takes the natural human love to the next level. It is opportune here to recall the basic teaching of Saint Thomas Aquinas, OP, on grace in general, that in our fallen state we need grace in order to heal our nature, in order to entirely abstain from sin and that grace presupposes nature (cf. ST I-II, Q.109, A. 2, 8).

A third grace proper to Holy Marriage affirms the indissoluble unity of the spouses. The holy vows of Holy Marriage are for life, "until death do we part." Perseverance, is difficult, but possible with God's grace.

A fourth grace proper to Holy Marriage is the sanctification of the spouses on their way to eternal life. When husband and wife are faithful to each other and to the holy vows of Holy Marriage, Heaven awaits them. To be sanctified is to be holy. The saints are those who lived holy lives and were repentant for their sins and died in a state of grace. (cf. CCC, 1661)

4.   Holy Marriage is not based only upon the emotions or feelings. The will plays a central part in the Sacrament of Marriage. If the bride and groom do not will to give themselves, each to the other, definitively, mutually, exclusively, then their vows have little traction and are just words. If there are "warm fuzzes" and passionate emotions accompanying the vows that can be great, no doubt. But what about "after the honeymoon"? Without the will to live the Holy Vows of Marriage there is no Marriage.

The classic expression in the Church is that "consent makes the Marriage." When the bride and groom exchange their vows this is also called the "exchange of consent." The bride and groom are also called in the formal language of the Church the "contractants" of the Sacrament of Marriage. The couple are the ones who exchange their consent, not their parents or friends or acquaintances, but this man and this woman vow, promise with God as a witness, fidelity all the days of their lives.

Part of the requirements for a valid exchange of the Holy Vows of Marriage is mutual self-giving. The idea here is not 50% + 50% but 100% + 100% from both the bride and groom with God giving the interest which is greater than 100% insofar as Heaven is in the cards for those who live out their lives faithfully to God and their vows.

A second part required for a valid exchange of the Holy Vows of Marriage is to will a definitive gift-of-self. Here, a classic Latin axiom come in handy: *nemo dat quod no habet* (no one gives what he doesn't have). In order to give yourself in Holy Marriage you must first be self-possessed (which is much different from being demonically possessed). Being a virtuous person, living the virtues, enables one to be "self-possessed."

A third component required for a valid Marriage requires it to be lived as a faithful alliance. Faithfulness includes but is not limited to the Marriage bed, which is sacred. There are other hours of the day when husband and wife are not in the Marriage bed, and they are called to be faithful then too. Not just Monday through Friday, not just on the weekends, not just 9:00 to 5:00 or 5:00 to 9:00 but 24 / 7.

Fecundity is a fourth component making up a valid Marriage. When the husband and wife live lives which bear fruit which will last they are fulfilling the will of the Lord (cf. John 15:16). Holiness and children are lasting fruits. Mother Church does not require husbands and wives to have 20 + children or only 1.2 children.

"The world" curses large families while Sacred Scripture recognizes them as blessings from God (cf. Genesis 22:17; 26:4; Psalm 128:6). (cf. CCC. 1662)

5.   When many people think about a 'public state of life in the Church' minds race immediately to Monks, Nuns, Brothers, Sisters, Bishops, Priests and Deacons. These are in fact public states of life in the Church, but not the only ones. Marriage establishes the spouses in a public state of life in the Church. Husbands and Wives in Holy Marriage bear public witness not only by the rings they wear but by their faithfully living out the Holy Vows of Marriage.

While there have been reasons for Holy Marriage to be celebrated clandestinely (the so called *droit du seigneur* comes to mind) normally Holy Marriage is celebrated publicly. One reason for this is so that all will be able to join in prayer for the new couple. Another reason is to avoid scandal, otherwise, people would not know the difference between those who are *viventes in peccatis / viviendo en pecado* (living in sin) and those who have received and are living the Sacrament of Holy Marriage.

Because of the dignity and importance of this sacrament, not only for the couple but for the Church and society, Holy Marriage is rightly celebrated liturgically.

While there are three (3) different categories of Holy Marriage: Sacramental (two Catholics or two baptized Christians), ecumenical sacramental (a Catholic and a baptized non-Catholic spouse), interfaith (a baptized Christian and a non-baptized spouse) the liturgical rite always includes the proclamation of Sacred Scripture and the exchange of consent through the Holy Vows. Optimally, Catholics get married in the context of the Nuptial Mass, which allows the new couple to receive together the Body of Christ in Holy Communion, which strengthens them for the journey they have undertaken together. Then, each subsequent time they approach the Altar together to receive Holy Communion their bond with Christ and His bride Mother Church is deepened as is their bond with each other.

Specific for the validity of Marriage for Catholics is that the Holy Vows be exchanged and the sacrament celebrated before the Priest or qualified witness of the Church (cf. *Code of Canon Law*, Canon 1108). This ensures the integrity of the sacrament. Bishops, Priests and Deacons are the ordinary qualified witnesses of the Church, while in mission lands Catechists often fill this role due to the dearth of clergy.

To further ensure the integrity of the Sacrament of Marriage and it's validity, Mother Church requires two further witnesses, who are often called the 'best man' and 'maid' or 'matron of honor.'

The gathered faithful, the assembly of the faithful, also play a role in the liturgical celebration of Holy Marriage. The participation of the congregation at a wedding is a pledge of prayer, not only for that day, but also for the long term, for the fidelity, health and well being of the couple. (cf. CCC, 1663)

6.   Consideration of three essential properties help us to recall and appreciate the sacramental signification of Holy Marriage. These are and have been counter cultural. When lived they change lives and cultures. When something is 'essential' that is to say it is necessary, like water for fish.

Unity is essential to Marriage. Polygamy and polyandry are incompatible with the unity of Marriage. In this we are reminded that Holy Marriage is that union between one man and one woman only, not a *many-wived man* or a *many-husbanded woman*. Monogamy alone is compatible with the unity of Holy Marriage. Sacred Scripture shows some of the bad consequences of sins against the exclusive unity of Holy Marriage (cf. Genesis 21:11; 35:22-26; 37:28; 1 Kings 11:7-12).

Indissolubility is essential to Marriage. Divorce separates that which God has united. Jesus Himself identifies the re-marriage of a divorced person as an adulterous situation (cf. Matthew 5:31-32). The Lord further clarifies that it was due to the hardness of hearts that Moses permitted a bill of divorce to be written (cf. Matthew 19:6-12; Mark 10:4; Deuteronomy 24:1-4). Fecundity (fruitfulness) is essential to Marriage. Refusal of fecundity (fruitfulness) diverts the conjugal life of its 'most excellent gift' the child' (GS, 50). God commanded our first parents to be fruitful and multiply, to fill the earth (cf. Genesis 1:28). Children, as a most excellent gift given in Holy Marriage, remind us that no one has a right to parenthood, although married couples have a right, naturally, to try. The child has the right to be born of the love and actual union of parents.

While the refusal of fecundity has taken on various forms, they are mostly united under the term contraception. Surgical (vasectomy, elective hysterectomy, tubal ligation), chemical (oral, injected), and barrier (diaphragm, condom) methods all contradict the meaning of the nuptial embrace and total gift of self. Neither Almighty God nor Mother Church require spouses to have 20 + children, nor are they restricted to 1.2 children (where does that .2 come from, a big toe?). Responsible parenthood recognizes the capabilities of the spouses and has recourse to *natural family planning* which utilizes the naturally occurring signs of fertility, and fosters growth in virtue.

Sometimes critiques are offered against Mother Church and her teachings concerning human sexuality: 'those celibate guys...' These always bring to mind my maternal grandfather who never personally suffering from cramps or the pains of childbirth, nevertheless, he helped many who did as an obstetrician and gynecologist and father of seven daughters. We expect our oncologists and cardiologists to treat those conditions, not to have necessarily have suffered from them. Pope Paul VI in *Humanae Vitae* addresses in a deep way these matters as does Blessed John Paul II in his *Theology of the Body*. (cf. CCC, 1664)

7.   Wholesale "no-fault" divorce and remarriage seems rampant in society today. A study of 1995 marital statistics published in 2001 by the Center for Disease Control (CDC) highlights marital success for those who complete the first ten years, while 1/5 of marriages end within five (5) years and 1/3 end within ten (10) years. This provides Mother Church the opportunity to recommit boldly to the sure and certain teaching received from Christ the Bridegroom regarding the indissolubility of Holy Marriage. Christ makes explicit the design and law of God regarding the indissolubility of Holy Marriage in Saint Matthew 5:31-32; 19:3-12 and Saint Mark 10:2-12.

The common axiom of jurisprudence is that we are "innocent until proven guilty." So too in the Church.

Once a couple legitimately exchanges the vows of Holy Marriage, they are presumed to actually be married. Non-Catholics are free to exchange their vows according to any legal form. Catholics are bound by *canonical form* in order to exchange the vows of Holy Marriage validly. This is what the *Catechism* means when addressing those who have a "living legitimate spouse." The legitimate spouses are those spouses who actually pronounced the vows, effecting that partnership of the whole of life, until death (without any recourse to crimes against the Fifth Commandment).

That the divorced and remarried are not separated from the Church should be a consolation. Whenever any of us sadly sin mortally, thereby leaving the state of grace, we do not thereby leave the Church. Acting badly, as if we have not been baptized, or confirmed, or married, or ordained... does not change the fact.

Saint Paul's exhortation to examine ourselves lest we receive the Eucharist unto our condemnation is not limited in it's application only to those who are divorced and remarried (cf. 1 Corinthians 11:27-29). Anyone who is sadly in a state of serious, grave, or mortal sin, does not have access to Eucharistic Communion. The Sacrament of Penance is the way to regain the grace lost by sin. Part of a good Confession includes the firm intention, with the help of God's grace to sin no more and to avoid whatever leads us to sin.

Those who are bound by the civil laws of marriage while bound by the law of Christ find themselves in an irregular situation at best.

Not all cases submitted to the Ecclesiastical Tribunals result in a declaration of nullity, in part because Marriage enjoys the favor of the law and once a valid Marriage has been established no one should put it asunder (cf. Matthew 19:6). While not having access to eucharistic communion those who are divorced and remarried, without a decree of nullity, are to lead their lives notably in educating their children in the faith, encouraging fidelity and holiness all the while. (cf. CCC, 1665)

8. The family home, with Holy Marriage as it's foundation, is the basis of 'the domestic Church.' Many of us may be familiar with our various Parishes (e.g. Holy Ghost, Little Flower, Saint Augustine, Saints Peter and Paul...) and even with the Church which is the Diocese (e.g. Knoxville, Louisville, Miami...) the *Catechism* draws our attention to the domestic Church. The Hebrew word *qahal* and the Greek word *ekklesia*, which are translated as "Church" mean a meeting or congregation or assembly. Holy Marriage is the sacred assembly, meeting, congregation of husband and wife. The blessing of children adds to the sacred gathering.

Married parents provide the first announcement of the Faith for the children.

Even before infants might be baptized they should hear and see, even if not understanding completely, the faith, by the love shown by their parents. By seeing the faith lived out daily by the parents the faith is taught to the children.

The stability of Holy Marriage makes the family a community of grace. The family home is filled with various graces: the baptismal graces of the parents and children; the grace of Confirmation and Marriage...

The stability of Holy Marriage establishes a community of prayer. Family prayer is a part of the life of the domestic Church: in the morning and in the evening; before and after meals... Some families pray the Holy Rosary together each day, with each member leading a different decade and voicing a particular intention. Before going to pray at Sunday (or daily) Mass normally we are at home. After praying at Sunday (or daily) Mass we often return home filled with the graces which prayer allows.

Married parents together with their children form a school of the virtues, human and divine. The curriculum of the school of the virtues includes knowing just what is a virtue. Virtue is a stable disposition to do good, even in the face of difficulty, with joy and ease (cf. ST I-II, Q. 55, a. 4).

There are many different sorts of virtue: Cardinal Virtues (Prudence, Temperance, Fortitude, Justice); Moral Virtues (Diligence, Humility, Generosity, Temperance, Brotherly Love, Patience, Chastity); Theological Virtues (Faith, Hope, Charity; cf. ST I-II, Q. 61-62). Prudence, allows us to do the right thing, at the right time, in the right way, for the right reason, as chief of the Cardinal Virtues (cf. ST II-II, Q. 47-56). Temperance (which is not abstinence) keeps us balanced from the extremes of excess or deficiency (cf. ST II-II, Q. 141-170). Fortitude, which is the strength to undertake and endure what must be done, is exemplified naturally by the United States Marine Corps, and supernaturally by the Martyr Saints (cf. ST II-II, Q. 123-140). Justice gives each their due, God, neighbor and self (cf. ST II-II, Q. 57-122). (cf. CCC, 1666)

The Priesthood of Jesus Christ was prefigured throughout the Old

Testament. Abraham offers tithes to God through Melchizedek

(Genesis 14) and the mysterious everlasting priesthood of Melchizedek

(Psalm 110:4; Hebrews 7:1-10) prepares for the High Priesthood of

Jesus Christ in which the ordained share by varying degrees.

ORDERS

1.   There are some people who say 'The Bible never mentions

Holy Orders." While literally that is true, the term "Holy Orders" is

not found in the Sacred Text, the reality permeates the Word of God.

This is so, primarily, because the Scriptures are primarily about Jesus

Christ who is the Great High Priest (Hebrews 9:11, 25). Saint

Augustine's axiom: 'In the Old the New lies hidden, in the New the

Old is fulfilled' is very applicable here.

Mother Church directs our attention to three passages of Sacred

Scripture which are instructive about Holy Orders, even if they are not

exhaustive (2 Timothy 1:6; 1 Timothy 3:1; Titus 1:5). The passages

come from the inspired pen of Saint Paul, two written to Timothy and

one written to Titus. Here we see a spiritual and paternal bond

between Apostle (whose successors are the Bishops) and disciples

(Timothy and Titus specifically). There are at least four things which

these three passages of Holy Writ teach us about Holy Orders: the rite,

the reality, two grades, apostolic origins.

206

While not an exhaustive blow by blow of the Rite of Ordination by any means, one of the significant gestures from the Ordination Rite is made explicit in 2 Timothy 1:6, namely, the imposition of hands. This ancient gesture signifies the transmission of the grace of the sacrament. Another technical term for it is 'epecletic' calling down the Holy Spirit. We see such a gesture in all of the Sacraments and throughout the Scriptures (cf. Exodus 9:29, 33; 17:11; 29:10-19; Numbers 27:23; 1 Kings 19:19).

The reality of Holy Orders, like all of the Sacraments, is that they are God's gift. God gives His grace, which is His powerful presence, in His Sacraments. While there is a natural right to Holy Baptism and Marriage for those who are properly disposed, no one has a right to Holy Orders and in this sense it is further a gift.

By mentioning 'Bishop' (1 Timothy 3:1) and 'Presbyters' (Titus 1:5) Saint Paul identifies two of the three grades of the Sacrament of Holy Orders. If we remember the Martyrdom of Saint Stephen, Saint Paul was familiar with the Deaconate as well (cf. Acts 6:5; 7:58-59)

That the Apostle to the Gentiles gave 'instructions' regarding these things serves to remind us of the apostolic origins of the Sacrament of Holy Orders which Christ first conferred upon them at the Last Supper. (cf. CCC, 1590)

2.   What is the role of a priest? To pray, to worship, to adore and serve God, this is the priestly task. Christians are a priestly people (1 Peter 2:9) and as such all the Baptized are called to pray, to worship and to adore and serve almighty God. Sociologically there have been priest (and priestesses) for millennia. When God formed for Himself a people, Israel, among the tribes were those of Levi, the priestly tribe. All of Israel was to pray, to adore, to worship God, but the Levites played a special part in all of this. So too the Priests of Jesus Christ. All the Baptized are called to pray even though the Ordained have a special role to play in our lives of worship.

There are two sharings in the one priesthood of Jesus Christ (Hebrews 3:1; 4:14-15; 5:5, 10; 6:20; 9:11): that by Baptism and that by Orders.

During the of the Year for Priests (2009-2010) the Church focused anew on the hierarchical participation of the ordained in Jesus' priesthood.

Whenever the Church maintains a phrase in Latin it is a reminder that it is a key phrase. *In persona Christi Capitis* is one such phrase. Used in reference to the ordained, the phrase means that a priest acts 'in the person of Christ the Head' of His body the Church. The *Catechism* reminds us that not only does the priest do what he does in the name of Christ (which is no small thing) but in His very person. The voice of this or that priest is heard, the eyes of this or that priest are seen but it is Christ who consecrates and Christ who absolves in the Sacraments: I absolve you... This is My body... spoken in the first person singular. In the celebration of the Sacraments the priest does not say: "In the Name of Jesus be absolved" nor does the priest say: "in the Name of Jesus be consecrated and changed into His body and blood"

When the police place us "under arrest" or a judge tells us we are "free to go" these are called 'effective utterances.'

What is said happens by the saying when those with the authority to say them do so. The 'effective utterances' made by the priest are effective because of the grace of Holy Orders and the power of God given in ordination that we all, head and members, might be absolved and receive Holy Communion. (cf. CCC, 1591)

3.   While there is only One New Testament Priest, Jesus Christ (Hebrews 3:1; 4:14-15; 8:1; 9:11), He allows a participation in His Priesthood in two ways, one by Baptism and the other by Holy Orders. The two are related in many ways: both come from Christ, both fulfil His will, both continue His saving work until He returns in glory at the end of time. They do differ however, according to the Lord's will. The Royal or Common Priesthood of the Faithful is for all of the baptized. Some men who have been baptized receive the Ministerial Priesthood of the ordained.

There is an essential difference between the two sharings in Christ's One Priesthood. When the word "essential" is used it is deliberate.

210

The Second Vatican Council solemnly taught in continuity with nearly 2,000 years of previous Magisterial pronouncements and Sacred Tradition that the 'difference' was not only of degree but essence (LG, 10). In Holy Orders, like Baptism and Confirmation, a 'character' is given, marking the soul as it were, for all eternity. One may act as if these sacraments were never received but that does not change the fact. It is to our eternal glory in Heaven or our eternal shame elsewhere how we live out the grace of these three sacraments. The technical term for the 'essential difference' is 'ontological change', the soul being the formal cause of our being (ontology is the science of 'being'), the change being the character received by ordination.

One of the consequences of the reception of the sacramental character in ordination is God's gift of a three-fold 'sacred power' whereby the ordained teach, govern and sanctify by divine right. What is taught is: Christ, crucified and glorified, His Gospel, His pending return in glory, what good we should do and what evil we should avoid...

Acts of governance include but are not limited to various temporal matters: where to have a Parish, a school, who will staff such institutions, hours of operation and the like... The sanctification occurs primarily through the administration of the Sacraments which are channels of God's grace.

The laity and the clergy (Bishops, Priests and Deacons) all together make up that one People of God who make up the mystical body of Christ which is Holy Church. Let us pray that all together with the various graces God gives each of us we will all be pleasing in His sight and ready to meet Him when he returns in glory to judge the living and the dead. (cf. CCC, 1592)

4.   The Sacrament of Holy Orders, like the other six Sacraments all date back to the origin of the Church which Christ founded.

We remember fondly the Lord's words to Saint Peter: "You are Peter and on this rock I will build **My Church**" (Matthew 16:18) and to Saul during his conversion "Why are you persecuting Me?" as he was still yet persecuting the Church (Acts 9:1-22). Christ Jesus our Lord instituted not only His one only Church but likewise her Sacraments by which He gives us His grace.

The one Sacrament of Holy Orders is exercised in three grades or degrees. There are three different ordination rites, each with prayers specific to the grade or degree received, each with specific vesture as further outward signs of the inward grace received. The three grades or degrees of the one Sacrament of Holy Orders are: Bishops, Priests, and Deacons.

Bishops receive the fullness of the Sacrament of Holy Orders. They are the visible source of unity of the particular Church (Diocese) entrusted to their care. They are the chief teachers and leaders in the Church with and under the guidance of the Bishop of Rome who is the Successor of Saint Peter.

During their ordination the Gospels are placed over their heads like a tent, covered by the Word of God. Their heads are likewise anointed with Sacred Chrism. Their insignia include the Pectoral Cross, the Miter, the Crosier, and the Ring.

Priests receive their faculties from their Bishops to offer the Sacrifice of the Mass, absolve the repentant, and anoint the sick and dying. The current rite of priestly ordination calls for the anointing of the palms of the hands with Sacred Chrism. The vesture of Priests includes the Stole worn over the Alb and under the Chasuble.

Deacons likewise receive their faculties from their Bishops and exercise ordinarily the ministry of the Word, especially the Gospel, and assist at the Altar especially the Chalice. The outward signs used by Deacons are the Stole worn diagonally under the Dalmatic. Deacons are not anointed during their Ordination but like Bishops and Priests they receive an imposition of hand prior to the prayer of consecration.

St. Ignatius of Antioch is cited by the *Catechism* to the effect that "without the Bishop, the Presbyters and the Deacons, one can not speak of the Church" (*Epistula ad Trallianos* 3,1).

For this faith he was martyred, ground like eucharistic wheat by the teeth of lions in AD 107. Let us pray that our Priests will be holy like Christ the great high Priest and bishop of our souls, following Him like Saints Peter, Paul and Ignatius (cf. Hebrews 3:1; 1 Peter 2:25). (cf. CCC, 1593)

5.   For centuries there was a controversy over what was the difference between a Bishop and a Priest. Both offer the Sacrifice of the Mass. Both Anoint the sick and dying. Both absolve the repentant. It was the Second Vatican Council (1962-1965) which solved and answered the question by teaching us that Bishops receive the fullness of Holy Orders in their Episcopal Consecration and Ordination (the Greek word *episkopos* means overseer, and Bishops oversee the Church founded and sustained by Christ) (cf. LG, 21).

It was at the Last Supper that Christ the Lord instituted both Holy Orders and the Holy Eucharist when He told the Twelve to "Do this in memory of Me." Jesus did not make the Apostles Deacons or Priests.

He made them overseers of His Bride, Mother Church, to teach, govern and sanctify those who follow Him who is the Way cf. (Matthew 26:26-27; Mark 14:22-24; Luke 22:19-20; 1 Corinthians 11:23-27; John 14:6). Bishops are the "Successors of the Apostles" and the Bishops continue this teaching, governing and sanctifying even until Christ should return in glory to judge the living and the dead, Bishops included.

While there was originally the body of the Twelve, the Bishops as successors of the Apostles now constitute a larger body (quantitatively) which we call the "Episcopal College" (don't confuse this with the University of the South at Sewanne). The term "Episcopal College" means the body of the Bishops united with and under the Bishop of Rome and never without him who is the head of the Episcopal College even as Saint Peter was head of the apostolic band (cf. Matthew 4:18; 8:14; 10:2; 14:28-31; 15:15; **16:16-19**, 22-23; 17:1-13, 24-27; 18:21-35; 19:27-30; 26:33-46;, 58, 69, 73-75...).

This is why the Pope, who is the Bishop of Rome and successor of Saint Peter has such an important place in the Church. In one sense he is a Bishop just like all the other Bishops. But as Bishop of Rome his authority and jurisdiction are not limited to the "Particular Church" which is the Diocese of Rome. In matters of faith and morals, all that we are to believe and all the good we are to do and evil we are to avoid (and repent if we sadly have fallen), the Pope teaches without any admixture of error. This charism or special grace is called "infallibility" and does not mean the Pope never sins (that would be "impeccability").

As followers of the Lord Jesus Christ in the one only Church which He founded and sustains we submit and unite our intellects and wills to that of the Successor of Saint Peter the Bishop of Rome and his brother Bishops who are with and under him even when scattered around the globe in their various particular Churches or Dioceses. (cf. CCC, 1594)

6.   When the *Catechism* teaches us about the Ordained Priesthood we are reminded that not only are the Bishops to be united with and under the Successor of Saint Peter, the Pope, but Priests similarly are to be united with and under their Bishop who is a Successor of the Apostles.

Sometimes when the term 'dignity' is used we often think 'stuffy' or 'arrogant.' This is foreign to the notion of priestly or 'sacerdotal dignity' as understood by Mother Church. The Office of the Ordained is one of dignity not because of the particular man who has been ordained, but more because of the One who is made present through the words and deeds of the ordained, Christ Jesus the Lord. Whether it is a Bishop or a Priest offering the Holy Mass or granting absolution in the Sacrament of Penance or Anointing the Sick the sacrament is no more or less valid or effective in itself, because it is Christ who is the primary actor in the sacraments. The *gloria ad extra* (external glory) is greater whenever the Bishop does what he does surrounded and assisted by his Priests.

The personal holiness of the Bishop or Priest likewise does not diminish the actual power of the sacraments but may effect one's willingness to approach the sacraments. We are not the only ones who would like to receive the sacraments from holy ministers, that was (and is Christ's desire too).

As a Bishops depend upon the Bishop of Rome for his office, the Priests likewise depend upon their Bishops for whichever Parish or Ecclesial Office in which to serve. So often all we know is the Parish Priest (Pastor) and his associates (if he has any). This is the 'normal' or 'ordinary' Ecclesial Office which Priests exercise. There are other Ecclesial Offices in which Priests often serve: School Chaplain and or Teacher, Vicars General, Judicial Vicars. These are particular 'pastoral functions' which presuppose the grace of Ordination, the 'being' of a Priest united to Christ the Head by the laying on of hands and prayer of consecration.

Together with and under the direction of the Bishops, Priests work as a body ('presbyterium') and individually in building up the 'Particular Church' which is the specific Diocese (or Eparchy in the Eastern Rites). The *Catechism* distinguishes between the specific portion of the People of God which is the Parish and the specific portion of the People of God which is the Particular Church. When treating the article of the *Creed* about the Church we will treat this in greater depth. (cf. CCC, 1595)

7.   One of the good fruits of the Second Vatican Council (1962-1965) was the restoration of the Deaconate in such a way that it was no longer just a transitional step towards Holy Priesthood.

One misnomer I have heard is to refer to the Deacons as "lay deacons." Nothing could be further from the truth. Those men who have been made Deacons, have been ordained and are in law and in fact clerics, sacred ministers of Mother Church.

While Deacons (like Priests) do not enjoy the fullness of Holy Orders as the Bishops do, unlike Bishops and Priests, Deacons are not ministerial nor hierarchical Priests. Deacons do not Anoint the Sick or Absolve the repentant in Confession. Likewise Deacons do not offer the Eucharistic Sacrifice even though their assistance to the Bishops and Priests at the Altar allows for a fuller expression of the mystery of the Church.

There are four aspects of service are highlighted by the *Catechism* when treating the ministry of Deacons: Word, Cult, Government, and Charity.

Even if the Pope or a Cardinal or a Bishop were at a Mass none of them would proclaim the Holy Gospel if there was a Deacon present. The proclamation of the Gospel is a special role fulfilled by Deacons. Similarly, when given faculties by the Bishop they may also preach during the various sacred liturgies. The proclamation of the Word of God is not limited to the Holy Mass and Deacons likewise fulfill this aspect of their ministry even in giving instruction, teaching the Faith to any and to all.

By the distribution of the Precious Blood and intoning various parts of the Sacred Liturgy, including the Prayers of the Faithful, the invitation to offer the Peace of Christ, to stand and to kneel, as well as the giving of certain blessings, Deacons fulfill their ministry of Divine Cult or Worship. The solemn leading of Eucharistic Exposition, Adoration and Benediction, the Liturgy of the Hours, Baptism and Marriage are likewise all a part of a Deacon's ministry.

Like Priests, Deacons may, with and under the direction of the Bishop, exercise governance in the Church and perform works of charity. Saint Lawrence, Deacon and Martyr is perhaps the most famous for both governance and charity, both in caring for the collection(s) in Rome and dispersing alms to the needy poor. (cf. 1596)

8.   One of the Seven Sacraments is Holy Orders. It presupposes the Sacraments of Initiation: Baptism, Confirmation and Eucharist as well as regular reception of Penance (as we are all in need of God's healing mercy).

There are some followers of Christ who do not accept that Christ the Lord instituted Seven Sacraments. We need to pray and work for the unity of Christians as Jesus did at the Last Supper (cf. John 17) and as has been a part of Ecumenical Councils throughout the years.

There is in the conferral of the Sacrament of Holy Orders the imposition of hands. The technical term for this is "epicletic gesture", a visible sign of the calling down of the Holy Spirit. In the three rites (bishops, priests, and deacons) the imposition of hand occurs on the head of the man to be ordained. In priestly and episcopal ordination all those having the same grade of Orders likewise impose hands as a sign of the fraternal bond. Each of the Seven Sacraments includes a calling down of the Holy Spirit: over the waters in Baptism, over the bread and wine in Eucharist, over those to be Confirmed, over the repentant in Penance, over the sick person in Anointing, over the husband and wife in Marriage, and over the bishops, priests, and deacons in Holy Orders.

The prayer of consecration asks God to give particular graces to the man being ordained.

The consecratory prayer asks God to help bishops be bishops and priests to be priests and deacons to be deacons. We need to all storm Heaven, not only on the day of ordination but always, that these graces will not be lacking, nor will they be spurned (tragically, we know only too well what the spurning of these graces looks like).

When a man has been ordained a Deacon, a Priest, or a Bishop there is a permanent "mark" made on his soul. This mark can never be taken away. For better (Heaven) or worse (Hell) the mark accompanies him, even as all who have been baptized and confirmed likewise receive indelible marks setting them apart for divine worship and service. Let us live so as to not be ashamed of the graces given us by Christ the Lord, so as to live with Him and all His Saints forever in Heaven. (cf. CCC, 1597)

9.   The Seven Sacraments are God's gift to the Church. These gifts are "packed" with grace, which is God's power and presence and more all at the same time. While we all like to receive gifts, the nice thing about receiving a gift is the gratuity of it.

There is no "right" to be ordained to the diaconate, presbyterate, or episcopate on the part of the man who is ordained. The sacrament is given, not only for the salvation of the one being ordained but also for the unbuilding of Mother Church that all might be saved.

While there are many of the sure and certain teachings of Mother Church which cause some perturbation, the "all male priesthood" is counter cultural in our day and age. Pope John Paul II, in continuity with 2,000 years of sacred Tradition, following the example of the early Church before the Greek (AD 1054) or Western Schisms (AD 1378-1417) has reaffirmed the teaching of Christ that the choice of Christ is normative not only in the use of water for Baptism, or bread and wine for Holy Mass, or Marriage being between one man and one woman, but likewise Holy Orders is conferred only upon some "baptized men (*viris*)" (*Ordinatio Sacerdotalis*, 1994). This is not to say that men or boys are holier or better than women or girls.

Manfred Hauke's doctoral dissertation (over 400 pages) *Women in the Priesthood?* (Ignatius, 1988) on the subject is very informative on this issue which he addresses on theological, anthropological, and historical grounds. Similarly, Aime Georges Martimort of happy memory (+2000), gives us further insight to this aspect of our saving faith in his *Deaconesses* (Ignatius, 1986).

Aptitude for ministry is not only the supernatural gift of faith but also applied reason as well as a humaneness which allows for qualitative interpersonal relations with the people of God.

When the *Catechism* points out the "right and responsibility" of the "authority of the Church" to call whichever baptized men to Orders it is an affirmation of the liberty of the Church. When various regimes have attempted to thwart the liberty of Mother Church they have sought to appoint clergy of their own choosing, imposing them on the faithful. The authority of the Church in the case of the call of Bishops ultimately rests with the Holy Father the Pope, while for the lower grades of Holy Orders, Priests and Deacons, the local Bishop is the human agent who makes the call on behalf of God.

226

Let us be sure to pray to the Lord of the harvest for an abundance of laborers in His vineyard which is the Church in the World. (cf. CCC, 1598)

10.   The *Catechism of the Catholic Church* is for the entire Church, not just the Latin Rite. At Holy Ghost Church in Knoxville, Tennessee, the Holy Sacrifice of the Mass has been offered with three distinct rituals: the ordinary form and the extraordinary form of Roman Rite and the Byzantine Ruthenian Rite. When treating the celibacy of Priests the *Catechism* focuses on the Latin West. The practice in the Catholic East allows for both Deacons and Priests to be married, but these marry before ordination.

While clerical celibacy is observed for Priests, is likewise true for Bishops who are taken from the ranks of the Priests. Even in the East where some of the junior clergy (Priests and Deacons) may be married, the Bishops, who have the fullness of Holy Orders, are only taken from among the celibate.

Clerical celibacy is the "normal" practice of the Latin Church.

Which is to acknowledge that there are other practices which are not the norm in the Latin West. Under what is called the "pastoral provision" there have been some who have ministered among other Christians before becoming Catholic who have likewise been married. These exceptions do not abolish the norm of clerical celibacy. Pope Paul VI published an encyclical on priestly celibacy in 1967 *Sacerdotalis Caelibatus* in which he said "Priestly celibacy" is a "brilliant jewel and retains its value undiminished."

No one has a 'right' to be ordained. Likewise, no man is to be forced to be ordained (even as no one should be forced to marry). Similarly, the promise or vow made before ordination is a freely made. Priests who belong to religious congregations, like the Benedictines or Dominicans or Jesuits publicly and freely make a vow of Chastity before they might be ordained. Secular Priests freely make a promise of celibacy before their ordination. Vows and promises both engage the 8th Commandment: How we are all to tell the truth and love the truth (another name for Jesus!).

Two motives are given for the promise (or vow) of celibacy (or chastity): Love of the Kingdom of God (where we are neither given nor taken in Marriage (Luke 20:34)); availability for service of others. The *Catechism* does not highlight here that Christ is the exemplar for the Priest and His bride is Mother Church. The technical term associated with the 'love for the Kingdom' above is "eschatological" because it has to do with life in Heaven which is anticipated in the here and now. (cf. CCC, 1599)

11.   Each of the Sacraments has a minister. In an emergency such as danger of death anyone can administer Holy Baptism so long as the water is poured over the head of the one to be baptized and the proper formula is prayed and the intention to do what the Church does is present. In Holy Marriage it is the couple, the husband and the wife (the bride and the groom) who are the ministers of that Sacrament. This being said, the ordinary minister of Holy Baptism is a Bishop, Priest or Deacon.

As for the Sacrament of Holy Orders, the minister is a Bishop. In order for a man to be ordained as a Bishop not only is there to be the Papal Letter calling him to the Episcopacy but at least three other Bishops are to impose hands upon the new Bishop's head to help show the unity of the Episcopal College. While other priests impose hands upon the head of a newly ordained Priest in the rite of priestly ordination, it is the Bishop who is the proper minister of both deaconal and priestly ordinations.

It is important to recall that the sacraments are "conferred" that is, given or administered. Receptivity is key here. One does not "take" the graces of Baptism or Eucharist or Confirmation, they are received, conferred upon us. The same is true in Holy Orders and the other Sacraments. Even though Priests and Bishops 'self-communicate' during Holy Mass, they can only do that because they have previously received those grades of Holy Orders.

There are three degrees or grades of the one sacrament of Holy Orders whereby the ministry of Christ is continued in the Church.

That the Bishops are the proper ministers of the Sacrament of Holy Orders in its three degrees (that of Bishops, Priests, and Deacons) is a further reminder that they possess by God's gift the fullness of the Sacrament of Holy Orders and they pass on, like the Apostles before them, the grace they themselves received.

Be sure to remember the clergy in your good prayers. Know that you are remembered in the prayers of the clergy, each time they approach the altar of God who gives joy to their hearts as we all together seek to do God's holy will day by day. (cf. CCC, 1600)